ETHNIC CHRONOLOGY SERIES
NUMBER 13

The Latvians in America
1640-1973

A Chronology & Fact Book

Compiled and edited by

Maruta Kārklis
Līga Streips
Laimonis Streips

1974
OCEANA PUBLICATIONS, INC
DOBBS FERRY, NEW YORK

Library of Congress Cataloging in Publication Data

Kārklis, Maruta, 1940-
    The Latvians in America, 1640-1973.

    (Ethnic chronology series, no. 13)
    Bibliography: p.
    1. Latvians in the United States--History.
I. Streips, Līga, 1936- joint author. II. Streips,
Laimonis, joint author. III. Title. IV. Series.
E184.L4K35   917.3'06'9193   74-13105
ISBN 0-379-00508-5

Manufactured in the United States of America

TABLE OF CONTENTS

iv

EDITORS' FOREWORD

This book surveys Latvian society in the United States of America. It gives available information on the amorphous groups of Latvians that came to the U.S.A. at the turn of the century as a result of Russian czarist oppression in their homeland, especially heightened by the uprisings of 1905. It traces the organizations, secular as well as religious, that these people set up, their press, and their relations to the new Republic of Latvia. It also gives some evidence that these immigrants were ultimately assimilated into American society, and only a few Latvian societies and churches survived until the midpoint of this century.

A completely different picture developed after 1950, when a large group of Latvians, about ten times the size of the earlier immigration, entered the U.S.A. under the Displaced Persons' Act. They too had fled Latvia to escape Russian oppression -- this time, in 1944, of the communist variety. Because of an identical recent past, this group already had some cohesion upon arrival in the United States. Several years of refugee life in Germany (1944/45-1949/52) had enabled them to organize on a secular and religious basis, geared to existence in exile, and within a dominant -- at that time German -- society. They had also been able to revive a rich cultural life, with schools on all levels of learning, and high caliber press, theater, ballet, and music, since many of Latvia's professional talents were among the refugees. This experience taught Latvians, like other nationalities under the same conditions, how to cope with a cultural minority status in their new homeland.

For this reason, as the book indicates, there was a newspaper, established in 1949, to greet many of the arrivals; the American Latvian Association in the United States, then, as now, the organization speaking for Latvians in the U.S.A., was formed as early as 1951; and religious life was being swiftly organized. That pinnacle of Latvian cultural and ethnic expression, the song festival, followed soon thereafter in 1953. Latvian life in the U.S.A., then, is well-organized, and permits a Latvian living here to participate in the best that the two societies have to offer. Many Americans (as well as Canadians and Australians) are beginning to recognize that the dominant society not only contributes to the national groups living within it, but, especially in the case of active ethnic minorities, also is enriched.

Like most Latvians arriving in the U.S.A., these displaced persons were political refugees. However, if the Latvian disembarking here before World War I was a socialist revolutionary, the Latvian who came in the 1950s was in determined opposition to communism, having personally experienced life under this system. Though these later refugees came from all levels of Latvian society, the middle class was heavily represented, including many professionally skilled and academically educated individuals. This was the group that had the most to fear from a Soviet take-over of their land. It is highly improbable that more than a percentage of them at best would have come to the U.S.A. had it not been for the political devastation of their homeland and its neighbors.

Because of language difficulties and formalities of qualifications, most of the displaced persons began their careers in the U.S.A. as unskilled laborers. Within ten years, however, they had acquired a measure of occupational advancement and prosperity. Very few, if any, Latvians had landed on welfare rolls, and the group emphasized higher education for their children. As a result, there are thousands of Latvians in responsible positions in government, academic institutions, and industry, as well as in American cultural life.

The organized life of the Latvians, detailed in this book, shows no signs of waning. As many, if not more, people attend Latvian events of various kinds throughout the U.S.A; leadership positions pass rather effortlessly into younger hands; Latvian supplemental school enrollments lately have shown an increase; books are being published, music written -- all hallmarks of a living society. And there is a future -- the bilingual youth adapted to two cultures, assimilated within one, yet choosing to cultivate the heritage of another as well.

The specter of what Russian imperialism is doing to Latvia and the diminishing number of Latvians in an ever more Russianized Latvia further motivate the maintenance of an alternate Latvian culture in the free world.

The Latvian society that operates within this framework, however, is by no means as large as the reported numbers of Latvians in the U.S.A. Many Latvian families have disappeared into the fabric of American society and abandoned the recognizable features of ethnicity. There are many reasons for this phenomenon. The two most prevalent, perhaps, are the desire not to be different and the pursuit of some materialistic or other goal, unencumbered by the complexities of biculturalism.

The dispersion of the Latvian society made the writing of this book difficult. There was no way to include all the contributions of Latvians in this country. Those who chose not to become involved with other Latvians have a tendency to leave no record with that society, nor do they necessarily show up as Latvians in American accounts of events. Similarly, the book frequently omits persons or undertakings that have been of importance only strictly within Latvian society because of constraints on the extent of the book.

The book, therefore, does not claim to be inclusive. Rather, it is a brief record of what the Latvians have done and are doing in the United States. The reader is referred to the English language publications mentioned in the book for more thorough treatment of many subjects only alluded to here.

The authors regret all omissions, assuring that omissions were not deliberate, but rather stemmed from incomplete or missing data.

The authors are indebted to Benno Abers, Osvalds Akmentiņš, Bruno Albāts, Dr. Edgar Andersons, Gvīdo Augusts, Zigurds Balodis, Alfrēds Bērziņš, John J. Germanis, Andrejs Jāgars, Dr. Peter P. Lejins, Roberts Līdums, Dr. Ilgvars Spilners, Anita Tērauds, Rev. Richards Zariņš, the late Aleksanders Liepnieks, and others.

Throughout this book, Latvian diacritical markings have been used, wherever possible. These are:

ā as a in car
č as ch in church
dž as j in jury
ē as ea in wear
ǧ no English equivalent; roughly similar to <u>dya</u>- as in woul<u>d'ya</u>
ī as ea in mean
ķ no English equivalent, roughly similar to <u>kya</u>-
ļ no English equivalent, roughly similar to <u>lya</u>- as in wil<u>l'ya</u>
ņ as n in new
š as sh in sharp
ū as o in move
ž as z in azure

In cases of persons better known in the United States by the anglicized form of their names, diacritical markings have been omitted and the anglicized spelling given. For example, the anglicized form Jacob Sieberg, rather than the Latvian form Jēkabs Zībergs, has been used.

1640   Some Latvians from Vidzeme arrived in the United States
                     together with Swedish and Finnish immigrants because their
                     native part of Latvia was at this time ruled by Sweden.
                     They joined Scandinavian settlements in Delaware and Penn-
                     sylvania.

Late 17th   Latvian colonists from Courland, experienced difficulties
Century   in settling in Tobago in the West Indies, then a colony of
                     the Duchy of Courland (1639-1693), and several times were
                     forced to leave the island. Many of them arrived in New
                     England and the southern coastal areas of the present day
                     United States.

1659-1661   The first Rector of the first high school in North America,
                     in Dutch New Amsterdam, was Dr. Alexander Carolus Cur-
                     sius, formerly a professor in Lithuania, presumably of
                     Latvian origin.

1687   A large Latvian group from Tobago settled in Massachusetts.

1688   An agreement of commerce and navigation between the Cou-
                     ronian governor of Tobago, Abraham Mann, and an Ameri-
                     can merchant company in Boston, headed by Samuel Shrimp-
                     ton, established a regular trade route of short duration be-
                     tween Boston, Madeira and Tobago, utilizing Couronian
                     ships and crews. Shrimpton had a commercial agent in
                     Riga, the largest port of Latvia.

1802   Georg Heinrich Loskiel (1740-1814) from Renda, Latvia,
                     leader of a religious revivalist movement in Vidzeme, and
                     the author of 400 Religious Hymns to Honor God (400 garī-
                     gas dziesmas Dievam par godu, 1790), emigrated to Penn-
                     sylvania and became a bishop of the Bohemian Brothers.
                     Some other pastors from Latvia, including Johann Reineke
                     and Johann Priedītis, were active in Wisconsin, Illinois and
                     other states prior to the American Civil War.

1849   A number of Latvian sailors went to California to prospect
                     for gold; there is no news of their fate. Only some place
                     names still denote Baltic origin. About the middle of the
                     century many Latvian sailors visited American ports and
                     later Latvian ships established regular routes to America.
                     A number of immigrants settled in the Midwest; the names
                     of several cities and towns, e.g. Livonia, Michigan, testify
                     to their past activities.

1861   Martin Bucin was one of the first casulaties of the American Civil War. He is thought to have been a Latvian sailor.

1888   August 15. A group of seven men, led by Jacob Sieberg (1863-1963), a master carpenter by trade, settled in Boston, Massachusetts. This date can be considered as the beginning of regular Latvian immigration in the United States. Sieberg organized the first Latvian Evangelical Church, and a secular society, and came to be known as "Father of Latvians." He was the editor of the newspaper Amerikas Vēstnesis (American Herald) and an author of seven books, among them a handbook for the study of English. This marks the beginning of documented and organized Latvian community life in the United States of America.

1889   December 24. The Boston Latvian Benefit Society, later the Boston Latvian Association, was founded at the initiative of J. Sieberg. This was the first Latvian civic organization in the United States.

1891   The Latvian Baptist parish was organized in Philadelphia, Pennsylvania, with a beginning membership of eleven persons. This group of Latvian immigrants was the first to establish a formal organization in the city of Philadelphia. The congregation has had an active, uninterrupted existence to the present, responding with charitable deeds to the turmoils of the twentieth century. Their donations went to Latvia, ravaged by World War I. After World War II they participated in various assistance measures to the displaced persons.

The first printed item in the Latvian language was published in the U.S.A. when J. Sieberg issued a public notice announcing a Latvian Lutheran church service to be held on July 5. This event preceded the establishment of a Latvian Lutheran parish in Boston a few years thereafter.

1892   February 22. The second Latvian civic organization in the U.S.A., the Philadelphia Society of Free Letts, was founded by nine young Latvians, most of them from Courland. The society's main goals are expressed in its charter: ". . . having associated themselves together for the purpose of maintaining and supporting a Society for the benevolent, charitable and educational work among its members; the primary object in view being to educate, elevate and assist its members so that they and their fellow countrymen may

become intelligent and useful citizens of this community."
Fritz Leschinsky was elected president, and continued to
fill this office for eleven years. The society staged an amateur theater performance in its founding year, which was
probably the first such Latvian event on the American continent. The society was incorporated in 1894, and its membership at that time was twenty-nine. This society has continued its existence and its varied civic functions to the
present time.

In this same year Latvian Relief Organization was founded
in Chicago.

1893   The first Latvian Lutheran congregation in America, the
Philadelphia Latvian Lutheran Church of St. John, still active in 1973, was organized. Until the arrival of an ordained
minister, Paster H. Rebane in 1896, the religious meetings
were conducted by the parishioners themselves. This practice was retained in the minister's absence as well, since
Rebane pursued missionary work throughout the North
American continent. Rebane's first Philadelphia service
on February 2, 1896, drew 115 church goers, who donated
$21.47.

The Latvian Workers' Association was founded in Boston.
This organization was welfare-oriented in the cause of so-
cialism. Its amateur theater group produced plays of a
"progressive nature" to raise proceeds for donations.
Among its successes was a 1909 production of Maxim Gorky's
Enemies. The performance drew an audience of 186 persons.

1894   The Boston Latvian Evangelical Lutheran Trinity Church was
established. The present-day Latvian Evangelical Lutheran
Church of Jamaica Plain dates its founding from this event.
This was the congregation organized by Jacob Sieberg in
1891 and served by Rev. Hans Rebane after 1896. The original name was retained by a splinter parish organized in
1902, likewise still in existence.

Charles Podin (born in 1872 in Erǧeme, Latvia, died in
1951, Long Island, N.Y.) came to the U.S.A. as a young
seaman. He studied for the ministry, was ordained in 1898,
and received an honorary Doctor of Theology degree in
1943. He was a minister for both American and Latvian
Lutheran parishes. He was responsible for the Latvian immigrant mission on Ellis Island from 1917 to 1933. Rev.

Podin was involved in many historical events that concerned
the Latvian community in the U.S.A.: in 1919 he participated in the Latvian delegations to President Harding and to
the Senate Foreign Relations Committee; during the 1930's
and 1940's Podin was minister of the Latvian Evangelical
Lutheran Church of New York and concerned with American
efforts on behalf of the displaced persons.

The first Latvians arrived in Alaska.

1896

The Boston Latvian community had grown to 296 persons
and was beginning to assume a central role in the cultural
life of Latvians in the United States. The first Latvian language newspaper in the U.S.A., Amerikas Vēstnesis
(American Herald), appeared in Boston. It was edited by
J. Sieberg until it merged with a paper called Amerikas
Atbalss (American Echo) in 1920. Originally it was a monthly, later a weekly, and finally a bi-weekly periodical with
a circulation of 250-500 copies. Its policy was oriented
toward ethnic and religious activities and it attempted to
counteract the melting pot philosophy of assimilation. Sieberg also published an annual Latvian Lutheran calendar
from 1897 to 1914.

From 1896 to 1903 the American-Latvian socialist newspaper Amerikas Latviešu Avīzes (American Latvian Newspapers) also appeared in Boston.

Pastor Hans Rebane (born in 1863, Valka, Latvia - died in
1911, Boston, Mass.), after completing theology studies in
Schleswig Holstein, Germany, arrived in the U.S.A. He
had left Latvia because of religious discrimination policies
of the Czarist government against Lutherans. Rebane was
of Estonian-Latvian parentage and spoke both languages.
In the U.S.A. he traveled 10,000 miles to seek out and minister to the scattered Baltic immigrants of his faith. His
missionary efforts in America were supported by the Missouri Lutheran Synod.

August Krastin (1859-1942), built his first automobile in
Cleveland, Ohio (see 1901).

1897

A Latvian lumberer settlement was begun in Lincoln County,
Wisconsin. The project was endorsed by Amerikas Vēstnesis (American Herald), and the first settlers were attracted from Chicago, Illinois and Philadelphia, Pennsylvania;

others came directly from Latvia. Urged by Hans Rebane, they formed the Latvian Evangelical Lutheran Church of Martin Luther. Two years later this rural congregation started construction of the first Latvian-built church on American soil. Heineman Lumber Company, the industry employing the settlers, provided the forty-acre site and materials for this building, which was completed in 1906.

The estimated number of Latvians in the U.S.A. was about 1,000.

1898   The American Latvian Social Democratic Association was founded in Boston. Its press organ, the scientific-literary monthly Auseklis. (Morning Star) appeared in Boston from 1898 to 1901, edited by Dāvids Bundža and J. Kundziņš, and was circulated also in Rīga, Latvia.

1900   The official census figures of 1900 indicate that there were 4,309 Latvians in the United States. This figure excludes numerous illegal entries, which are known to have taken place. The rapid immigrant increase reflects Czar Alexander III's religious and cultural repressions against minorities, as well as the economic hardships, which the subjects of his empire were forced to endure.

Pastor Hans Rebane carried his mission across the continent, visiting Latvians in South Dakota, California, Oregon, and Manitoba, Canada.

Frederic Sander lectured at Harvard University, Cambridge, Massachusetts. With his sister, he wrote an English primer for Latvian immigrants.

1901   August Krastin patented a new gasoline engine for automobiles. His Krastin Automobile Company produced both gasoline and electric cars. Krastin also constructed refrigerators, improved agricultural machines and various electrical devices.

1902   There were now seven Latvian Lutheran parishes in the United States: in Boston, New York City, Philadelphia, Baltimore, Cleveland, Chicago, and Lincoln County, Wisconsin. These were all a direct result of the activities and travels of Pastor Hans Rebane.

The literary-political socialist monthly Proletārietis

(The Proletarian) was launched in Boston, in 1904 it transferred to Zurich, Switzerland, then back to Boston, and
from 1912 to 1917 it was published in New York. It was
edited by J. Kundziņš, K. Siliņš, Jūlijs Vecozols, and
others.

From 1902 to 1905 the Latvian Baptist monthly Amerikas
Latvietis (American Latvian), edited by F. Huns and J.
Kalise, was published in Philadelphia.

1904   The Philadelphia Society of Free Letts (founded in 1892) purchased its first building for $3,000.00 on North Third Street.
This gave its members new impetus for participating in the
life of the society. English, mathematics and drawing
classes were arranged. Choral singing and literary discussions flourished in addition to amateur dramatics, which
was most popular. The society's troupe later visited New
York Latvians with its performances, and staged up to five
new productions in a single year. The society founded a library that today houses more than five thousand volumes
and contains numerous rare editions from the turn of the
century.

From 1904 to 1906 the journal Jaunais Amerikānietis (The
New American) was published in Boston.

Fritz Freidenfeld (b. 1886-   ) arrived in Boston from Latvia. He was active in the social and literary pursuits of
the Latvian community. He translated American literature
for Latvian publications, but accepted the realities of the
melting pot, urging rapid cultural assimilation of second
generation Latvians.

Jānis Šmits (1877-1929) came to the U.S.A. Šmits managed
the Latvian collection at the Chicago Public Library from
1913 to 1929. He was an author of short stories as well.

1905   This was the year of unsuccessful revolution in Latvia,
against Russian repressions both economic and cultural.
Because of severe Czarist reprisals, about five thousand
young Latvian socialist revolutionaries fled their homeland
and began to arrive in this country. The number of Latvians
in the U.S.A. doubled.

The Philadelphia Society of Free Letts expressed its sympathy with the revolution in Latvia, and raised money to support the anti-Czarist efforts.

From 1905 to 1917, a period of intensive Latvian activity followed the arrival of this socialist immigrant wave to urban centers of the U.S.A. Periodicals and books were published in greater numbers, local groups held theatrical events, concerts, and lecture meetings. Latvians actively participated in the American labor movement and held political demonstrations against the Czarist regime as well as the capitalistic system.

From 1905 to 1907 the moderate American Latvian Social Democratic party acted independently from other, more radical groups. It was organized in Boston prior to the wave of new immigrants, and would soon affiliate itself with the American Socialist party.

1906   The Latvian socialist newspaper Strādnieks (The Worker) was published in Boston, later in Fitchburg, and circulated to three thousand copies three times a week. Originally it was edited by John Klawa, then by John Ohsol, Frederik Rosin and J. Klawa again. It ceased to exist in 1919. A journal Jaunais Prometejs (The Young Prometheus) also appeared in Boston in this year.

Membership of the Philadelphia Society of Free Letts increased by 47 new arrivals from Latvia - political refugees who were fleeing Czarist reprisals for revolutionary activities. This socialist element overwhelmed the earlier membership, and the society assumed a politically leftist orientation, which it retained until 1950's.

Mīce Niedze arrived in New York from Latvia. She had begun a stage career in Riga and was to become one of the most popular actresses of the Latvian immigrant theater in the U.S.A. Among her earliest New York roles were the leads in Nebēdne meitene (Naughty Girl) by Aspazija and Zagļi (Thieves) by Rudolfs Blaumanis. Both were produced by the New York Latvian Society Auseklis (Morning Star). Niedze continued to play in similar productions for over thirty years in a total of some four hundred different roles. In New York these shows were staged at the Naronij Budov Czechoslovakian Hall. Latvian theater troupes frequently exchanged guest performances among Boston, New York and Philadelphia. Despite its popularity, this kind of theater remained amateur. Participants prepared the shows in their free time, often after putting in a full day's work as domestics and laborers. Other prominent names of the Latvian theater in New York include the directors J. Sauleskalns (Stage name Latvis) and A. Bērziņš; the actresses Ance Zībergs, Vilija Jansone-Slosberga, Lesija Matisone, and Elza Stāls; and the actors Alberts Munkāns, Paulis Rausks, Džims Blaus and Apsitis-Rozentāls.

Milda Salnais (1886-1970), convicted for revolutionary activities in 1905 and sent for life imprisonment to Siberia, came to the United States through Switzerland, after a successful escape from Siberia. She toured Latvian colonies and gave lectures. Upon returning to Latvia in 1917, she became associate director of the Latvian Telegraph Agency, LETA, as well as the Latvian correspondent for the Associated Press. In 1937, she moved to Sweden, where she was press attache to the Latvian Legation; she later worked for American and British newspapers.

Kristaps Jānis Bitners (Christopher John Bittner, 1883-1962) came to the U.S.A. In 1932 he received a Ph.D. degree for his dissertation on the social heritage of Latvian immigrants to the U.S.A. From 1938 to his death in 1962 he taught at the Western Ontario University in Canada.

Augusts Pinepuks (1876-1942) came to the U.S. He later graduated from the Chicago Conservatory of Music. Pinepuks was a composer and also director of the New York Latvian Choir and Orchestra.

Cinematographer John Dored (born in 1881 in Latvia) joined the Pathe Freres Studios. In 1911 he returned to Latvia and managed to film a number of historic Russian events: the March, 1917 revolt in Russia, Lenin's funeral, the Noble/Wilkins polar expedition, Dolfuss' assasination, etc.

The Latvian settlers of Lincoln County, Wisconsin, completed and inaugurated their church building.

From 1906 to 1908 the number of Latvians in the entire forest region of northern Wisconsin grew to an estimated maximum of two thousand. Some settlers had purchased land and cleared it for farming. There were about two hundred farms ranging in size from several tens of acres to more than one hundred acres. A few still extant farm buildings in this region show distinct similarities to rural architecture in Latvia. Subsequently, the history of this unique

Latvian settlement in America was to be one of inevitable
decline. Community discord arose between earlier settlers
and the revolutionary arrivals. Modern economic factors
also contributed to its dissolution. In a few decades, the
timberlands became depleted and small farms obsolete
through advancing mechanization. More and more Wisconsin Latvians abandoned rural Lincoln County for city life
and assimilation into the American society.

1907   The newspaper Brīvā Tribūna (The Free Tribune), edited
by K. Honold, was published in New York until 1908.

John Ohsol (1878-1968), a social activist, arrived from Latvia. He had been one of the founders of the Social Demo-
crat party in Latvia and the first editor of the leftist newspaper Cīņa (The Struggle). He led political activities of
Latvian socialist immigrants and edited for a time the periodical Strādnieks (The Worker). He received a Ph.D. degree in business administration from Harvard University
in 1914. Later, he worked for many years as a civil servant
in Washington, D.C.

1908   The Philadelphia Latvian Lutheran Church of St. John was
operating a Sunday school, choral group, and even an orchestra. Its Easter service this year attracted three hundred church-goers. Pastor H. Rebane was the part-time
minister of this thriving congregation, one of eight under
his guidance at the same time.

A precedent-setting legal proceeding in Chicago established
the right of two Latvian revolutionaries, J. Puren and K.
Rudovics, to receive political asylum in the U.S.A. Their
extradition had been demanded by Russia because of alleged
criminal acts during the 1905 revolution.

From 1908 to 1911 the Latvian anarchist publication Brīvība
(Liberty) was published, first in New York and later in
Paris.

1909   Kārlis Ulmanis (1877-1942?), the future president of Latvia,
graduated from the University of Lincoln, Nebraska, with
a B.S. in agriculture. He came to the U.S.A. to avoid re-
pression by Russian authorities and returned to Latvia during World War I. Many policies of Ulmanis' presidency
reflected his acquaintance with American ways. He initiated
the 4-H Club and Arbor Day activities, which Latvians es-

poused enthusiastically. Most important were the innovations he introduced in agriculture and dairy farming. These
innovations turned Latvia into a ranking European exporter
of dairy products. Ulmanis' proposal of 1933 for constitutional reforms in the Republic of Latvia included a president elected by popular vote, similar to the United States
election procedures. In 1940 Ulmanis was arrested and deported to the Soviet Union, where he reportedly died in 1942.

From 1909 to 1913 a series of short-lived ethnic periodical
publications appeared in the Latvian language: "Pērkons"
(Thunder) until 1911; a publication of satire and social criti-
cism: Dekadentu gaisma (The Decadents' Light). Apskats (Review), and others. The Latvian press was kept
alive by about twenty active writers, some of whom published poetry as well. They were all born in Latvia, however, and no American-born Latvians followed their traditions.

1910   Because of the sudden 1906 increase in membership, the
Philadelphia Society of Free Letts (founded in 1892) purchased
larger quarters in a building which the organization still oc-
cupies today. Its historic site faces the house where Edgar
Allen Poe wrote "The Raven," and is adjacent to the Philadelphia German Society, one of the oldest German civic organizations in this country.

Jack London and other American public figures spoke out
against the mistreatment of J. Vecozols, a Latvian journalist jailed in Boston upon his arrival from Switzerland to
serve as editor of Proletārietis (The Proletarian) in the
U.S. The Russian Consul had demanded Vecozols' arrest
because of an alleged bank robbery in Russia. Vecozols
proved his presence in Switzerland at the time of the robbery, and the crime was subsequently attributed to one Joseph Stalin.

1911   Hans Rebane died on December 18 of an illness brought on
by his excessive travels between the scattered parishes he
served.

The well-known botanist Oswald Tippo was born. In the
1960's he was the provost and chancellor of Massachusetts

University, and also the editor-in-chief of the American
Journal of Botany.

1912   Latvian writer Haralds Eldgasts (1882-1926) traveled in the
U.S.A. His best book Pa okeānu (Over the Ocean) resul-
ted from this trip.

Only two Latvian language periodicals were in publication
in 1912: the socialist Strādnieks (The Worker), and the
moderate nationalist Amerikas Vēstnesis (American Herald). Both were to outlast a rush of new, short-lived publications, all of which expired in 1917: Jauna Tevija (New
Fatherland), an illustrated Baptist magazine edited by A.
Fūrmanis in Philadelphia, Pennsylvania from 1913 to 1917;
Proletārietis (The Proletarian), a socialist paper edited
by J. Vecozols in New York, New York from 1914 to 1917;
Prometejs (Prometheus), a fine-arts, illustrated periodical edited by E. Kaktiņš and John Ozolin (Burtnieks) in San
Francisco from 1915 to 1917; Darba Balss (Voice of Labor),
a socialist paper edited by Vilis Dermanis, John Ohsol, and
M. Salnā-Kļaviņa in Fitchburg, Massachusetts from 1916 to
1917. From 1915 to 1916 there was a Latvian language periodical for every six thousand Latvians in America. These
publications were expressly one-sided, representing specific religious or political trends.

1913   A Latvian Baptist parish in Bucks County, Pennsylvania, was
founded.

Anna Enke was the first Latvian woman in the U.S.A. to receive an academic degree from the University of Chicago.
Later she was a professor of romance languages at several
academic institutions.

Eduard Stockman, a ship mechanic, was on the first American vessel to sail through the Panama Canal. Stockman was
an active member of the Latvian community in Boston.

1914   Six thousand Latvians were now living in Massachusetts.

This was the most active year of theater performances for
the Boston Latvian dramatic groups - there were twenty
stage productions.

From 1914 to 1919 a mandolin quartet entertained the Latvian community of Boston on numerous occasions. Its members were Earl Rosenwald, John Treis, Edward Rosenwald, and Arwed Brachman. Brachman played with the Boston Symphony for many years.

1916   During the war, more than two years in advance of the historical event, <u>Amerikas Vēstnesis</u> (American Herald) was advocating the idea of an independent Latvia. Principal writers on this anticipated issue of Latvian self-determination were: Ernests Minka, Krastins, and J. Līdumnieks.

1917   The Latvian War Association was founded in Boston at the initiative of J. Sieberg. The association supported the American war effort by selling Liberty bonds. It also affirmed its support for the gradually evolving possibility of independence for Latvia. With conclusion of the war, this association ceased its activities. One year later, it merged with the American National Latvian League, which espoused an American-Latvian effort to further Latvia's independence.

Latvian socialists objected to U.S. involvement in the war against Germany. Several demonstrations were held in Boston.

Henrietta Ābele-Dermanis graduated from Simmons College in library science. After the Revolution she returned to Russia and worked in the library of the Soviet Academy of Science in Moscow. During Stalin's purge she was condemned to forced labor and died in Vorkuta in 1938.

Mikhael Kasak received his M.D. degree from St. Louis University. He was born in 1884 in Latvia, to which he returned in 1922, but re-emigrated to the U.S.A. in 1925. He held the post of director of Milwaukee County Psychiatric Hospital. His wife Lauma founded the Wisconsin Latvian Association in 1951.

1917   From 1917 to 1919 two hundred and fifty Latvian communist revolutionaries repatriated from the U.S.A. to Russia after the Revolution. Several of them came to hold responsible positions in the Bolshevik regime, but most of them were to perish in the Stalinist purges of the 1930's.

1918   April 6. Boston held a spectacular Liberty bond parade celebrating the anniversary of America's entrance into World

War I. Fifty-six Latvians joined this patriotic extravaganza
under their own banner. This was probably the first time
that Latvians took part as an identifiable ethnic group in an
all-American mass event.

At the initiative of J. Sieberg and other members of the Latvian War Association, the American National Latvian
League was founded in Boston to promote autonomy and independence for the people of Latvia. This event took place
on September 7, two months before the actual proclamation
of an independent Latvian republic was made in Rīga on
November 18, 1919. The Amerikas Vēstnesis (American
Herald', notably the journalist J. Līdumnieks, hailed those
events in stirring editorials. Politically moderate Latvians
identified with the ideas of the league and soon the organization had chapters in New York, Philadelphia, Chicago and
Cleveland.

The first American Latvian collection of poems, Maldi un
Valgi, was published. The author, Jānis Burtnieks, later
published in Japan a book in English on Latvia and became
a professor of literature. He also served as correspondent for the English language section of Americas Atbalss (American Echo) when he published literary essays
and translations of Latvian poetry, notably works of Jānis
Poruks and dainas, the folk poetry of Latvians.

Many Latvians enlisted in the U.S. armed forces, and
many of them fought in the U.S. Army and Navy during
World War I.

From 1918 to 1920, the Latvian baptist illustrated journal
Drauga Balss (Voice of a Friend) appeared in New York,
and later, from 1945 to 1948, reappeared again, edited by
Rev. K. Purgailis.

1919   On January 3 to 5, the First American National Latvian
League Congress was held in New York, with delegates
participating from Boston, New York, Philadelphia, Chicago
and Cleveland. This Congress chose Charles Ozols as a
representative of American Latvians to the Paris Peace Conference, where self-determination for Latvia would be an
issue for discussions. J. Kalniņš was appointed Latvian
Consul in New York. On behalf of Latvians in the U.S., the
American National Latvian League sent the resolutions of
its Congress to President Wilson. They appealed for his

support of Latvia's independence and for Allied recognition of delegates from the Provisional Government of Latvia at the Peace Conference in Paris.

Because of their desperate, war-devastated circumstances, the people of Latvia appealed for aid from their countrymen abroad in the United States. Both money and medical supplies were urgently needed. The prime minister of Latvia, Kārlis Ulmanis, formerly a student in the United States, twice sent telegraphic appeals, personally, confirming the need of his people.

The Latvian National League of Boston donated a three thousand-dollar truck to the Latvian Red Cross and several thousands of dollars in money and clothing. The year before, Jacob Sieberg had raised money through the Amerikas Vēstnesis (American Herald) and sent $997.00 in support of Latvian battalions, fighting to liberate their land from foreign military troops. He had also sent $1,824.00 to the Latvian Provisional Government for relief of war victims.

Herbert Hoover, the future United States president, visited Latvia during his European tour as director of the American Relief Administration in order to personally view the war devastation. Hoover developed a friendly relationship with Kārlis Ulmanis, the Latvian prime minister, and was later influential during Harding's administration in gaining U.S. de jure recognition for Latvia

Walter M. Chandler, a member of the U.S. House of Representatives, visited Latvia and reported his observations to the U.S. Congress.

August 29. Delegates of American Estonians, Latvians, Lithuanians and Ukrainians conferred on behalf of their native lands with the U.S. Senate Committee on Foreign Relations under the leadership of Senator H. C. Lodge of Massachusetts. Latvians were represented by delegate F. Podiņš, who submitted filmed documentation of war devastation in Latvia.

September 14-16. A congress of the four above-mentioned nationalities was held in New York. The participants envisioned an alliance between their newly independent native lands and wished to further American support for them through U.S. political recognition and trade agreements.

Though historically of little effect, this congress did popularize the fact that distinct nationalities within Russia strug-
gled to retain their ethnic identity and achieve political independence.

September 14-16. The second Congress of the American
National Latvian League was held in New York. This event
was marked by the first display in America of the newly
adopted red-white-red official flag of the Republic of Latvia.
A Latvian student fraternity's tricolor (Fraternity Lettonia)
had been used as the national symbol up to that time. The
central committee of the organization was transferred to
Philadelphia. This chapter had a membership of 140, subscribing to the slogan "Latvia, and all for Latvia." Among
the leading members of the Philadelphia chapter were Christopher Roos, Dr. J. Eiman, K. Rāviņš, G. Āboliņš, J.
Sirms, P. Steiks, J. Meistars, Ernests and Anna Minka.
The central committee of the league also published a bulletin, Latvija Amerikā (Latvia in America).
ca).

Dr. Christopher Roos published three thousand copies of a
brochure in English, "Latvia and the Russian Catastrophe,"
to introduce the American public to Latvians and their fight
for self-determination.

November 18. Latvians celebrated the first anniversary of
Latvia's independence at Faneuil Hall in Boston. Andrew J.
Peters, mayor of Boston, also attended.

Dr. Christopher Roos (born in 1887 in Kuldīga, Latvia) became chairman of the central committee of the American
National Latvian League. Dr. Roos had arrived in the
U.S.A. in 1906 and he had studied at the University of Wisconsin. Professionally, he headed the bacteriology department at the Mulford Biology Laboratory in Philadelphia,
Pennsylvania. Dr. Roos was the spokesman of the official
delegations and the author of formal appeals submitted by
the league to the U.S. government, in support of independence for Latvia.

Dr. John Eimann (born in 1886 in Talsi, Latvia) served as
vice-chairman of the central committee of the American
National Latvian League. Dr. Eimann is a graduate of the
Medical School of the University of Pennsylvania. He served
as head of the pathology department of Philadelphia Presby-
terian Hospital and taught at the University of Pennsylvania.

John D. Akermann (born 1897 in Rundāle, Latvia, died in
1971 in Minneapolis, Minnesota), a major name in U.S. aeronautics, left Latvia for the United States. From 1916 to 1917
he had been a flyer in the French Air Force during World
War I. He studied aviation at the University of Michigan,
and later taught aeronautics and airplane construction at industrial institutions, and from 1929 he taught at the
University of Minnesota. In 1931 he was appointed dean of
the School of Aeronautics at the University of Minnesota.
He was also aviation consultant for Boeing, and the official
investigator from 1942 to 1971 at the National Defense Department Research Center. He built all-metal transport
planes, tailless craft and rotors. He donated motor designs
to Latvia, to further aviation in his homeland. He was the
author of numerous publications and technical literature in
his field.

1920

Charles Ozols (1882-1941? in Siberia), engineer and diplomat,
was designated by the government of Latvia to represent its
interests in matters of trade and commerce with the U.S.A.
(prior to the establishment of formal diplomatic relations
between the two countries). In this capacity he negotiated
the first treaty between Latvia and the American Relief Association, dealing with medical and financial aid to Latvia,
ravaged by World War I. Between 1918 and 1920 he had published extensively in the American press (the New York
Times and elsewhere) about Latvia. He was assigned as a
diplomatic representative of Latvia to Russia from 1923 to
1929. In 1941 he was forcibly deported from Latvia to the
Soviet Union.

April 17. A Latvian delegation participated in the U.S. In-
ter-racial Council. This council was set up to defend the
image of immigrant communities discredited during a prose-
cution of communists by the U.S. Department of Justice.
Thirty-two nationalities participated and protested discrimination against the foreign-born.

From 1920 to 1922 Christopher Roos and K. Rāviņš edited
Amerikas Atbalss   (American Echo) in New York. It had
a circulation of three hundred and contained an English language section. This paper was ethnically oriented and supported Latvian independence and the efforts of the American
National Latvian League. It was the primary moderate Latvian press organ in the U.S.A. to counteract the militant
socialist publications.

November 18. On the second anniversary of Latvia's independence Congressman Walter Chandler addressed Latvians
in New York.

Christopher Roos published twenty-five thousand copies of
a speech by the Honorable Walter M. Chandler and widely
circulated it in the U.S.A. and abroad.

A split in the ranks of the American Latvian socialists had
begun the year before, causing reorganization throughout
the Latvian communities. Radical socialists affiliated themselves with the Communist party as the Latvian Workers
Union, which was formed in New York and evolved a membership of 1,000 throughout Canada and the U.S.A. They
published a radical socialist newspaper Strādnieku Rīts
(Workers Morning) until 1935, when it was banned and the
American Communist party dissolved. For some four hundred New York socialists, the split resulted in four different
new organizations. In Philadelphia, the formerly culturally
engaged Latvian branch of the Socialist party, active since
1908, ceased to exist. Its non-communist members joined
the Society of Free Letts.

Jānis Blumbers published a collection of poems, Slavas
dziesmas (Songs of Praise).

The Boston Joint Latvian Baptist and Lutheran Choir received
first prize of $200.00 at the fifth International Music Festi-
val held in Symphony Hall for the song "Sēju jauku rožu
dārzu" (I planted a lovely rose-garden).

Rev. J.A. Freijs, a Baptist minister, arrived in the U.S.A.
from Latvia.

1921   May 30. The American National Latvian League sent a commission, led by Christopher Roos, to visit President Harding and to petition for de jure recognition of Latvia. J. Sieberg, J. Eimann, P. Volmar, E. Stockman, G. Neiman, L.
Sēja, A. Kundziņš, and J. Ozols were present at the meeting.
They were accompanied by Walter Chandler.

October 29-November 12. The American National Latvian
League represented Latvians in the New York Exposition
called "America's Making," where twenty-nine other nationalities participated. Latvians exhibited hand-crafted furni-
ture (Balodis), hand-loomed textiles, and paintings by Vil-
helms Purvītis, the noted Latvian landscapist.

Congressman Walter M. Chandler visited Latvia. He bore
the official congratulatory message of American Latvians
upon the achievement of independence for Latvia. It was
delivered to Jānis Čakste, president of the Constitutional
Convention of Latvia.

The government of Latvia sponsored a concert tour of U.S.
cities by the two best Latvian opera soloists - Ada Benefelde
and Pauls Sakss. This was intended as a gesture of appre-
ciation for the support received from countrymen abroad
to rehabilitate World War I devastation. Latvian communities in Boston, Philadelphia, and New York received the artists enthusiastically, and they sang to full houses. These
concerts represented one of the few times that Latvian immigrants in America experienced direct cultural contact
with their homeland.

Jānis Stelmachers, president of the National Youth Association of the Republic of Latvia, toured the U.S.A. to famil-
iarize American Latvians with circumstances in their newly
independent native country.

Edward Liedeskalnin began building his Corral Castle near
Miami (Homestead, Florida). His construction, now a major tourist attraction, was erected in the anticipation of his
fiancee's arrival from Latvia. She never came. Liedeskalnin died in 1951.

1922   July 27. The U.S. Government under President Harding extended de jure recognition to Latvia, Estonia, Lithuania
and Albania. Amerikas Atbalss (American Echo) hailed
the event with huge headlines. American Latvians received
telegrams of gratitude from the Latvian government.

January 1. Arturs Ļūļa (1882-1941?) started his activities
as the first Latvian career consul in New York; he later received a Ph.D. in law from the University of Chicago, and
he was Latvian Consul General from 1926 to 1930, and
Charge d'Affairs of Latvia from 1927 to 1935. He was deported to Siberia in 1941.

Ludvigs Sēja became the first Latvian minister to the United
States and represented Latvia in Washington until 1927.
Latvia also had honorary consulates in Los Angeles, Indianapolis, New Orleans, Philadelphia, San Juan, San Francisco,
accredited consulates in New York and the Consulate General
in Washington, D.C.

The New York Latvian Youth Club (later the New York Latvian Club) was organized by a moderate group, who wished
to commemorate Latvian independence day, an activity
shunned by other clubs with socialist membership. Consul
A. Ļūļa supported its patriotic policy. Leading members
of this group were Emilija Podin and Harijs Lielnors. The
Club met at the YWCA's International Institute in Manhattan,
and pursued drama and musical activities.

Arvēds Kundziņš (1891-1950) was appointed secretary of the
Latvian Legation. In 1927 he was licensed as an architect,
and in the ensuing years designed a number of municipal
buildings in Washington, D.C.: the Municipal Center Building, Police Court Building, Municipal Court Building, Juven-
ile Court Building, Center Public Library Building: He also
initiated in Washington, D.C., the functional school building that is widely acclaimed today.

The American Latvian National League held its fifth congress
in Boston and did not reconvene again. The sole remaining
moderate Latvian newspaper, Amerikas Atbalss (American Echo), also ended publication in this year. Both events
were symptomatic of a general decline of interest in the
Latvian subculture and rapidly increasing assimilation of
Latvians in America.

1923 About one-fifth of the Latvians in America at this time chose
to return to their homeland, now a liberated, independent
republic. Among them was Rev. Jānis Steiks.

Rev. Jānis Steiks (born in 1855 in Umurga, Latvia, died in
Rīga, Latvia) had spent seventeen years in the U.S.A. between 1906 and 1923, but had experienced disillusionment
for his hope of evolving a strong, nationalistically-minded,
ethnic Latvian colony in America. Steiks had been associated with the General Council of the Evangelical Lutheran
Church in America.

The Latvian Library Society was organized in New York.
This society rented a building at Madison and 126th Street,
and established a lending library, including publications
from Latvia. Its facilities were sublet to new immigrants
as temporary first living quarters in the United States. An
excellent chorus' sang for a time under the auspices of the
society, conducted by a well known Latvian composer, Jānis
Vītoliņš. The society's flourishing activities were greatly

reduced by the economic crush of 1929. It lost the building along with the enthusiasm of its membership.

Latvian poet Hugo Stikhewitz (1878-1966) started his career in the U.S.A. Under the name of Hermit he published seven collections of poems in English and Latvian, including Hermit's Religion, My Americanism, Love Poems, and Tev, Latvija, from 1923 to 1935.

From 1923 to 1935 the radical socialist newspaper Strādnieku Rīts (Workers' Morning) was published in Boston.

1924

From 1924 to 1934 Latvian educational and athletics organization Prometejs (Prometheus), headed by John Grava, was active in Philadelphia. Grava (1895-) was named chief chemist at Sharp and Dohme Company in 1934. Grava remained a leading personality of the Philadelphia Latvian community even after the displaced person immigrant wave arrived. He held office in the Society of Free Letts during the 1950's and is now an honorary member of that organization.

Henry Brown developed a nonstinging strain of the honey bee by crossing Italian and Cypriot strains. He gave some of these bees to his native Latvia.

1925

Anna Rūmane-Ķeniņa (b. 1877 in Jelgava, d. 1950) arrived in New York on a lecture tour. She made a second U.S. visit in 1928. Educated in Geneva, she had served as Baltic advisor to the press section of the French foreign ministry. She was also a Latvian press representative in Paris, where she published Revue Baltique in 1918-1919. Rūmane-Ķeniņa was professor of economics at the Pacific Lutheran University, Tacoma, Washington and the mother of the well-known Latvian composer Tālivaldis Ķeniņš, presently residing in Canada.

1926

Gustav Dancis launched a moderate-nationalist newspaper from New York, Amerikas Latviešu Ziņas (American Latvian News), but it closed the same year for lack of financial means.

The government of Latvia appointed J. Sieberg honorary Latvian Consul of Boston. He held this post for ten years. He was also awarded a Tri-star Medal of Honor by Latvia for his efforts on behalf of Latvian culture abroad in the United States.

Fifty-four Latvians sailed from New York on a vacation to Latvia, to attend the seventh General Song Festival in Rīga.

Jānis Vītoliņš (1886-1957), composer and wind instrumentalist, arrived in New York. He was a graduate of Moscow and Latvian conservatories and he had played in several orchestras in Rīga between 1920 and 1926. In the U.S.A. he joined various Broadway orchestral groups that performed in the Grand silent movie theaters of New York: the Paramount, the Capitol, and the Roxy. With the introduction of sound movies, Vītoliņš became one of three thousand musicians left unemployed. He returned to Rīga in 1931. Vītoliņš' important contribution to the Latvian community activities in New York was the direction of a musically sound choral group, which he conducted during his stay at the Latvian Library Society. Later in Latvia he composed some nineteen chamber quartets, piano sonatas, and one rhapsody.

From 1926 to 1933 the Latvian journal Auseklītis (The Morning Star) was published in Boston.

The Latvian Communist newspaper Amerikas Cīņa (The Struggle of America) was published in Chicago (until 1929), later in Boston and New York, edited by J. Palls, O. Priedin, J. Brigaders and K. Dirba.

1927   Krišjānis Nātriņš, Krišjānis Sproģis and Jānis Blumbergs published a collection of poems, Dzimtenes dzintari (Ambers of the Homeland).

Alfrēds Kalniņš (1879-1951), organist and pianist and a graduate of the Conservatory of Petersburg, arrived in the U.S.A. He was an organist in New York until he returned to Latvia in 1933. Kalniņš became popular also outside Latvian circles in New York. His compositions for organ were performed in Samuel A. Baldwin's organ concerts. Kalniņš is also considered the father of Latvian opera, having composed the first national classical opera Baņuta in 1919, followed by Salinieki in 1926 and a ballet Staburags in 1939-1941. He also composed numerous songs, and works for choirs, orchestra, piano and organ.

1928   April 20. The Treaty of Friendship, Commerce and Consular Rights was signed between the U.S.A. and Latvia in Rīga.

This year was historically the most successful for the Latvian community in Philadelphia, prior to the displaced person immigration to the U.S.A. after World War II. The Society of Free Letts alone sponsored twenty-two different events, including five amateur theater productions. Other active Latvian organizations in the city included the educational group Prometejs, the Latvian Music Society, and the Workers' Protection Association. The above were united in the Latvian Council of Progressive Organizations, which coordinated their projects and gave impetus to Latvian community life in Philadelphia for the five succeeding years.

The Latvian Evangelical Lutheran Church of Jamaica Plain, Massachusetts, purchased their own church.

November 17. On the tenth anniversary of the Republic of Latvia, New York Latvians held a joint Independence Day celebration. Participating organizations were the New York Latvian Club, the Latvian Library Society of New York, and the First Latvian Baptist Church of New York. Speakers included Rev. J.J. Kvietiņš, Rev. P. Steiks, K. Ķivuls, K. Karols, H. Lielnors, Anna Rūmane-Ķeniņa. The festivities concluded with a concert by Alfrēds Kalniņš, Biruta Kalniņa, and a choir conducted by J. Vītoliņš.

The Latvian Consul, A. Ļūļa, compiled an English language travel guide, Latvia, Guiding Facts with Hints for Travelers, with bibliography and illustrations, published in New York.

J. Birznieks published a collection of poems, Varavīksna (Rainbow).

1929   March 29. The first full program concert in America devoted to a repertoire of Latvian folk songs took place in New York. Accompanied by her father, composer Alfrēds Kalniņš, Biruta Kalniņa gave a recital of twenty-two folk songs arranged by him. The concert was introduced by A. Kalniņš' lecture on the nature of the Latvian folk song. English translations of the texts were provided. The soloist was dressed in a symbolic stage costume created for her by artist Niklāvs Strunke in Rīga, incorporating stylized elements of Latvian folk costumes. In addition to the Latvian press, this concert was favorably reviewed by the Evening World and New Yorker Staats Zeitung.

John Daugman, a Baptist minister, came to the United States. Daugman received a doctorate in theology from Harvard in 1933; he was also the minister of the Latvian Baptist Church of Boston, and a professor at Mt. Ida and Gordon Colleges in Boston, Massachusetts. He edited the Latvian journal Ausma (Dawn) from 1942 to 1945.

1930   Census figures indicate a high rate of assimilation of Latvian immigrants in the United States. Of 38,091 persons who declared themselves Latvians, 17,418 were born in the U.S.A., but 20,673 had arrived from Latvia. Of the latter, about sixty percent were U.S. citizens, and ten percent had declared their intentions to become naturalized. Only thirty percent of the Latvian immigrant families were still using the Latvian language. On the other hand, however, Latvians were not taking full advantage of the U.S. immigration quota. During the period of 1930-1939, 956 people came here from Latvia. Nearly three times as many would have been admitted.

January 13. The treaties of arbitration and conciliation were signed between the United States and Latvia in Rīga.

Several prominent scholars at the University of Latvia, of either professional or graduate student rank, received Rockefeller Foundation grants for research in the United States: Arnolds Spekke (1930-1931) in history, and Arnolds Aizsilnieks (1932-1933) in economy, both for post-doctoral work; and Jānis Vālbergs (1931-1933) in law, Peter P. Lejins (1934) in criminology, and Leonīds Slaucītājs (1936) in geophysics, all for graduate study. In their subsequent careers, each of these scholars has risen to international prominence because of scientific achievements that have significantly furthered knowledge in his respective field. In addition to their scientific contributions, two of them, Prof. Lejins and Prof. Spekke, have played personal roles in Latvian society with direct influence upon the history of Latvians in America.

Biruta Kalniņa gave her second New York recital, accompanied by composer Alfrēds Kalniņš. The program included familiar German and American composers, but also introduced for the first time in the U.S.A. the compositions of Jānis Mediņš. She sang three arias from Mediņš' opera Uguns un nakts (Fire and Night): Laimdota's "Nāc, nāc," Spīdola's "Dzer manu dzidrumu" (Drink of my clarity), and

"Maigums un spēks" (Tenderness and Strength). Favorable reviews appeared in the New York Herald and New Yorker Volkszeitung.

The Latvian Lutheran Church of St. John, assisted by the Mission Synod, purchased a building in West Philadelphia. The congregation remodeled it, adapting the facilities for church services and other public gatherings.

Jēkabs Graudiņš and M. Meiers began building skyscrapers in New York City.

1931   The Latvian consulate in New York was among the earliest tenants of the newly opened Rockefeller Center. Historically, the consulate goes back to 1919, when Jānis Kalniņš received the appointment as consul during the American National Latvian League Congress. The consulate was subsequently led by Artūrs Ļūļa, Nikolajs Āboltiņš and Vilibalds Kalējs.

1932   April 12. A concert of Latvian music took place in New York under the auspices of the Roerich Center for International Art. Soloist Biruta Kalniņa-Tripodi sang Latvian folk and art songs in English translation. Alfrēds Kalniņš accompanied and presented some of his own piano compositions. He also introduced the program with remarks about Latvian music. The Latvian consul general, Artūrs Ļūļa, was guest of honor. The Roerich Center presented citations to both performing artists.

1933   A. Wesson organized a group excursion to Latvia on the occasion of the eighth General Song Festival, held in Rīga, Latvia once every five years. They sailed on the Battery. Rev. Ch. Podin of New York was among the tourists. In Latvia, he was received by President Alberts Kviesis and decorated with Latvia's Tri-Star Medal of Honor. Rev. Podin was inspired by the festival, which was reflected in subsequent Latvian community activities he led in New York.

Ādolfs Legzdiņš (born in 1899), an engineer, came to the United States. Since 1940, he has been a professor of mines and metallurgy at the University of Missouri.

The Latvian Evangelical Lutheran Church of Bucks County, Pennsylvania, purchased its own church.

1934   November 17. New York radio station WJZ devoted a two
            hour and fifteen minute broadcast to Latvian programming
            in honor of Latvian Independence Day, November 18. An
            address by the consulate general, A. Ļūļa, was heard.
            Biruta Kalniņa-Tripodi sang Latvian songs.

1935   Dr. Alfrēds Bīlmanis was appointed minister plenipotentiary
            of Latvia to the United States of America. In Latvia he had
            served as the head of the press division of the Latvian for-
            eign ministry, later as minister of Latvia in Moscow, then
            in the United States. After World War II he was second in
            command in the Latvian Diplomatic Corps immediately af-
            ter Mr. R. Zariņš in London. He kept his post in the United
            States until his death in 1948.

            The Latvian Society of Chicago, Illinois was founded.

            The American Latvian Workers Union separated from the
            American Communist party.

1936   Andrew Edgar Murneek was elected president of the Society
            of Plant Physiology. Dr. Murneek was an author and editor,
            and he taught at the University of Missouri.

1937   Dr. Anatols Dinbergs (born in 1911) was appointed vice-con-
            sul in New York; in 1941 he was appointed attache to the le-
            gation of Latvia in Washington, D.C., and was the director
            of its consular activities.

            Victor Babin (born in Moscow, died in 1972 in the U.S.A.)
            held his New York debut as duo-pianist with his wife, Vitja
            Vronski. As a pianist and composer, he received his de-
            gree in 1928 at the Conservatory of Latvia, studying under
            the Latvian composer Jāzeps Vītols. Later, Babin was a
            student of Artur Schnabel in Berlin. Babin taught music at
            Santa Fe, Aspen, and other summer schools of music.
            From 1961 to 1972 Babin was the director of the Cleveland
            Institute of Music.

1938   The Latvian American Chamber of Commerce was founded
            at the initiative of Rudolfs Sillers, consul of New York, to
            promote trade relations between the United States and Latvia.

            September 4. The last service was held at the Latvian-
            built church in Lincoln County, Wisconsin. Regular ser-
            vices had ceased long before and did not resume after this

special commemoration of the Latvian settlement's fortieth
anniversary. Rev. Pudsell had come from Philadelphia to
conduct the same service twice - in Latvian and in English.
The Latvian version of that day's song sheet contains the
history of the community and its church: ". . . built to
serve as a monument for generations of Latvian Lutherans
in America." In the 1950's, the abandoned building was
sought out by some displaced persons as an object of historical curiosity with an ominous symbolism. The church bell,
a gift to this congregation by one Kaucis in 1906, was transferred to the Latvian Evangelical Lutheran Church of Minneapolis when its first home was demolished.

The Latvian tanker Hercogs Jēkabs (Duke Jacob) sailed on
its first trip to the U.S.A. and stopped at the port of New
Orleans. Vilis Veldre, correspondent for Brīvā Zeme (Free
Land), a Rīga newspaper, was on board and wrote press
reports about this trip and the United States.

1939   Besides the Latvian legation in Washington, D.C., there
was a Latvian career consul in New York, and honorary
consulates in Cleveland, Chicago, Philadelphia, St. Louis,
Indianapolis, Pittsburgh, Galveston, New Orleans, Los Angeles, San Francisco, Portland, Milwaukee, and Seattle.

With the outbreak of World War II, Latvian Socialist organizations were revived to pursue pro-Russian propaganda,
benefiting from the general antifascist atmosphere of the
country. The Communist Unity Club worked to discredit the
efforts of moderate Latvian groups in America, who were
appalled by the threatening Russian occupation of Latvia.
Events leading up to it date from October, 1939, when the
government of the USSR forced mutual assistance treaties
on Estonia, Latvia and Lithuania.

During September and October the USSR-pressured demands
for military bases in Latvia, Lithuania and Estonia received daily front-page coverage in the U.S. press. It was
generally acknowledged that freedom in these countries had
been jeopardized, and that their independence would be of
short duration.

Because of ominous threats to world peace and Latvian sovereignty, the Republic of Latvia could not participate in the
New York World's Fair. To fill the gap, Gustav Dancis organized Latvian Day at the fair with participation of the local

Latvian community. On August 26th, a choir of thirty-
seven singers, led by Oswald A. Blumberg, held a concert
of classical religious music in Latvian at the fair's Temple
of Religion. The Latvian composer Pinepuks conducted the
choir in his own choral work "Daile un saules stars" (Grace
and Sun-Beam). Rev. Charles Podin gave an address entitled
"Nation's Awakening, " introducing the public to his little
known Latvian nation. The concert met with such success
that the choir was invited to return to the temple for a second performance one year later.

Oswald A. Blumit (died in 1971), arrived to represent Lithuanian and Latvian Baptists at the World Baptist Conference
in Atlanta, Georgia. Rev. Blumit remained in the U.S.A.,
actively campaigning against Communist oppression of his
people. Author of several books, he is best known for
countless speaking appearances and organizational activities
in Boston commemorations of Captive Nations Week.

Jānis Leskinovičs (1894-1940?), wrestler and European champion in heavyweight and Greek-Roman wrestling, returned
to Europe from the U.S.A., where he had participated in
some 150 free-style wrestling matches. He disappeared
during the early part of World War II.

1940   June 17. Soviet armed forces invaded Latvia, Estonia and
              Lithuania, instating outright occupation of these countries.

              July 23. The U.S. Secretary of State, Sumner Welles, is-
              sued a declaration condemning Soviet aggression and their
              occupation of Latvia, Lithuania and Estonia. The U.S. of-
              ficial position on this issue has remained the same to this
              day.

              The U.S.S.R. demanded that Latvian ships in U.S. waters
              return to Soviet ports. These orders were accompanied
              by threats endangering the seamen's families back home,
              and some ships complied. Most of the ships and their crews
              remained, however, and served in the U.S. Navy.

              August 25. The second Latvian Day at the New York World's
              Fair was held. The concert at the Temple of Religion pre-
              sented New York choral groups augmented by the Baptist
              Youth Choir from Philadelphia, led by Helen Stanislaw. The
              program followed a format similar to that of the first Lat-

vian Day. Rev. Podin spoke this time on "The Secret of
Latvians' Unconquerable Soul." As this event was taking
place, Latvia was under Russian military occupation, her
people terrorized by mass deportations. 1940 is known in
Latvian history as the "year of terror."

October 6. Baltic Day was held at the New York World's
Fair, at the Court of Peace. The Latvian flag was displayed
there, as it no longer could be in Rīga, Latvia. The diplomatic representatives of the three occupied Baltic countries,
Estonia, Latvia and Lithuania, spoke at this event. A concert of folk and art songs of the three nations followed.

The Latvian communist and radical socialist newspaper
Amerikas Latvieši (American Latvians) was founded in Boston. It was edited by J. Liepiņš and later by J. Leimanis
and E. Mauriņš.

1941 Elza Žebranska (born in 1903), a Latvian soprano trained
in Latvia and France, had her debut at the Metropolitan
Opera in New York as Venus in Wagner's Tannhauser. L.
Melchior and Lotte Lehmann sang the title roles, with
Erich Leinsdorf conducting. In Latvia, Žebranska had been
on the faculty of the Latvian Conservatory of Music, and
soloist at the National Opera in Rīga. She had visited the
U.S.A. in 1937, giving recitals in New York and Philadelphia. Since 1939 she has resided in the U.S.A. In 1946-47
she sang with the San Francisco Russian opera and she conducted a voice studio in New York in the late 1940's and
early 1950's.

September 22. The Latvian Relief Organization was established and led by H. Lielnors to provide assistance for Latvian victims of World War II, especially refugees, who
were beginning to flee from their native land. The Latvian
Relief Organization cooperated with the American Red
Cross and various religious organizations.

Ludvigs Ēķis (1892-1943) was appointed economic advisor
to the Latvian legation. During his years in the U.S.A.,
Ēķis published two books in English: Latvia's Struggle for
Independence, and The Truth about Bolshevik Atrocities in
Latvia.

From 1941 to 1945 seventeen Latvian merchant vessels
served the cause of the Western Allies with a total of

55, 879 tons. Eleven Latvian ships with a total of 37, 066 tons were lost. Eight Latvian vessels were in U.S. service and only two of them survived the war. Several hundred Latvian seamen lost their lives for the Allies during the war. Considerable numbers of Latvians also served in the American Army, Navy, and Air Force.

1942   The Latvian tanker Ciltsvairs was sunk by Germans in U.S. waters. This was the first of the Latvian ships to be lost. Life magazine reported the tragedy. Lost soon thereafter were six other Latvian warships including the Apgars, Everalda, Everelga, and Regents.

A joint committee of Latvians was established in New York, to propagandize Latvian nationalist viewpoints and to counteract communist efforts. J. Lenovs, K. Karols, and K. Purgailis were active in this movement. They published a monthly newspaper Drauga Vēsts (News from a Friend) until 1948.

During 1939-1942, Dr. A. Bīlmanis, the Latvian envoy to the U.S.A., published Latvia as an Independent State for American readers, depicting the first Soviet occupation of Latvia, as well as the early part of the German occupation. Within a short time, Dr. Bīlmanis and the Latvian legation issued fifty publications about Latvia in English.

The American Baltic Society of New England was founded to popularize their native music. Among the founders were Latvians, J. Sieberg and Rev. C. Selmer, one Estonian, Ludwig Jucht, and one Lithuanian, Honorary Consul Oswald Shalna. The society sponsored three concerts annually. The Baltic Concert Series of 1957 was reviewed by Harold Rogers, music critic of the Christian Science Monitor.

May. The Philadelphia Society of Free Letts celebrated its fiftieth anniversary. An American choir sang Latvian folk songs; the Latvian minister to the U.S.A., Dr. A. Bīlmanis, and guests from other Latvian communities attended.

1943   Dr. Arthur Osol (1905), a pharmacist, became the dean of the Philadelphia College of Pharmacy and Science. He had edited several professional journals and major reference works, among them Dispensatory, and Practice of Pharmacy. From 1933, when he received his Ph.D., to 1937, Dr. Osol served as the League of Nations specialist in opium analy-

sis. During World War II he was in charge of the production of pharmaceuticals for the U.S. armed forces.

1944   In order to outline the illegal aspects of the forcible Soviet
take-over of Latvia, the Latvian legation in Washington,
D.C. published Latvian-Russian Relations, edited by Dr.
A. Bīlmanis. It was a compilation of official documents
and treaties between the Latvian republic and the Soviet
Union.

The Latvian Relief Organization, together with Estonian
and Lithuanian groups, submitted a memorandum to President Roosevelt asking him to reject Soviet demands for the
forcible repatriation of Baltic refugees from Western European countries.

1945   An order was issued by the Allied forces stating: "Latvians,
Estonians and Lithuanians can not be repatriated to the Soviet Union unless they affirmatively claim Soviet citizen-
ship." This order saved most of the Balts from forcible
repatriation. Without it there would have been no "Latvian
DP's" and no present-day Latvian community in the U.S.A.

From 1945 to 1948, the Latvian Relief Organization conducted
lobbying activities in the U.S. Congress for the passage of
special immigration laws, permitting DP's to enter the
U.S.A. under a special immigration quota.

1946   A catalogue was compiled by Latvian Relief Organization
listing American relatives and friends of Latvian displaced
persons (DP's) in Western Germany. This data greatly fa-
cilitated the subsequent immigration of Latvian refugees to
the U.S.A.

December 28. Latvian baritone, Viktors Stots, was the first
DP immigrant artist to hold an independent recital in New
York City at Town Hall.

1947   George Marshall, the U.S. secretary of state, again declared that the U.S.A. did not recognize the annexation of
the Baltic states by the Soviet Union. All subsequent U.S.
administrations, including the present one have reiterated
this view.

The first Latvian World War II refugees crossed the Atlantic Ocean from Sweden to the U.S.A., landing in Florida.

Others followed to New England in the Gundel, the Skagen, and the Masen. The arrival of such refugees gained much public attention, and they were referred to as "Latvian pilgrims." Senator John F. Kennedy supported granting them immigrant status, despite their unusual entry into this country.

Rev. A. Klaupiks was appointed director of the welfare and relief section of the international Baptist World Alliance. He arrived in the U.S.A. in 1950, where he started publication of the Latvian Baptist periodical Kristīgā Balss (Religious Voice).

Edgar Andersons, historian, was elected president of the Latvian College Students' Association.

1948   Dr. A. Bīlmanis, the Latvian envoy in the United States, died.

Public Law No. 774 of the eightieth Congress of the U.S.A., known as the Displaced Persons Act, was signed by President Harry S Truman. The essential provisions of this act enabled the extraordinary admission of displaced World War II victims into the U.S.A., without regard to the current quota limitations, but charging them to future quotas of their countries of birth up to 50 percent of the quota per year.

The movement of refugees in Europe during and immediately following the war can be summarized as follows: at the conclusion of hostilities, some 8,000,000 refugees of various nationalities were left on German soil. About 7,000,000 returned to their homes by 1947. By the end of 1948, another 315,000 had been resettled elsewhere. Some 40,000 immigrated to the U.S.A. under President Harry S Truman's directive of December 22, 1945; the remainder, about 850,000, could be broadly separated into the following categories:

1) Forced laborers from Poland, the Ukraine and Yugoslavia; these people had been brought to Germany during the war, but refused to return because of the communist take-over of their native land.
2) Persons from the Baltic States (Latvians, Estonians, and Lithuanians), who fled the advancing Soviet Army in 1944 and firmly refused to return to their occupied native lands.

3) Persons returning to or entering Germany: those who fled Nazism to elsewhere; refugees, mainly Jews, fleeing post-war anti-Semitism in Poland, Rumania and Hungary.

For this book, distribution of groups 1 and 2 is of major interest. The International Refugee Organization (IRO) cared for 125,000 Balts, 225,000 Poles, 86,000 Ukrainians, and 25,000 Yugoslavs. Furthermore, another 300,000-400,000 displaced persons lived in Germany, but not under the auspices of IRO. A part of these, too, were Latvians, Estonians and Lithuanians. For these people some special assistance was required, because they could neither be absorbed into the German economy of that time, nor resettled elsewhere in Europe in large enough numbers. Of this necessity the Displaced Persons Act was born.

Under this act displaced persons eligible for immigration were those who on or after September 1, 1939 and on or before December 22, 1945 entered Germany, Austria, or Italy and resided in Germany or Austria on January 1, 1948. Further, these persons had to be victims of war circumstances; they had to be qualified to enter the U.S.A. under its immigration laws and be suitably employed.

During the two fiscal years following the passage of the act, 202,000 persons were to be admitted without regard to national quotas. Among them were about 45,000 Latvians. The regular immigration quotas for Latvians were very small. Conditions in Latvia during the post-World War I period had seldom forced emigration to other countries, such as was necessary in Ireland during the potato famine. Thus, the number of Latvians in the U.S.A. previous to World War II was extremely small, and during the entire years of Latvian independence (1918-1940) only 666 Latvians emigrated to the U.S.A. Comparing this number with the approximately 200,000 Latvians seeking refuge after the Second World War, it is evident that most Latvians left their country only when the occupation government made life at home unbearable. In fact, only 3 percent of Latvians who fled the advancing Soviet armies returned home after the war.
The nature of this immigrant group is significant for their adaptation to the American life. These were people who had fled communism because of its specific threat upon their persons, property, and way of life. Many had been the po-

litical, religious, educational, artistic, scientific and business leaders of their country. Their professional competence extended through the entire range of learned professions.

Their entry into the U.S.A., however, was contingent upon a guarantee of employment. A personal contract was required between every adult immigrant and a specific employer in this country. With very few exceptions, the Latvian immigrants found employment as part of the unskilled work force in the U.S.A. Because of language barriers, they began work as janitors, agricultural laborers, dishwashers, construction workers, etc., without regard to their educational background or professional experience.

Rev. Oswald A. Blumit toured the U.S.A. in search of sponsors to guarantee Latvian refugees employment, thus enabling them to enter this country. Since the war, Blumit had been active in arranging various forms of U.S. aid to DP's in Belgium and Germany.

Mārtiņš Straumanis was appointed professor of metallurgy at the University of of Missouri. He had been director of the Analytical Chemistry Laboratory of the University of Latvia. He had been a Rockefeller scholar, and with A. Ieviņš developed a new method for X-ray crystallography.

From 1948 to 1950 the Latvian national newspaper Tālos Krastos (At the Far Shores), edited by Edgars Brūveris and Edgars Andersons, was published in Philadelphia.

1949   Jules Feldmans was transferred from his diplomatic post in Switzerland to become the new charge d'affaires at the Latvian legation in Washington, D.C. The accredited Latvian diplomats in the free world were the only remaining representatives of the government of the Latvian republic, since the country had been forcibly incorporated into the Soviet Union.

The Latvian newspaper Laiks (Time), the major regular Latvian press organ in the U.S.A., began publication in Brooklyn, N.Y. Published by Helmārs Rudzītis, the paper appears twice weekly; Kārlis Rabācs was named its senior editor. The publisher, Rudzītis (1903-), began a New York publishing house, Grāmatu Draugs, under the same name as his once highly successful Rīga concern, started in 1926.

The chief editor of Laiks, Kārlis Rabācs (born in 1903 in
Latvia), has been with the paper since its founding date.
In Latvia, Rabācs had edited Ventas Balss (Voice of River
Venta) from 1933 to 1934 and was on the staff of Rīts (Morn-
ing) from 1934 to 1940. In Germany he was the editor of
Latvija (Latvia) from 1946 to 1949. He also published one
volume of poetry, Vasara (Summer), in 1931. In the 1970s,
Artūrs Strautmanis became chief editor.

The Wisconsin Latvian Society, with 307 members, was
founded by Mrs. Lauma Kasak. From 1946 to 1948 Mrs.
Kasak had been extremely active in supplying care packages
to the displaced persons in West Germany. Through her
efforts in arranging immigration affidavits, about 600 Latvian DP's families were able to settle in Wisconsin.

Efforts of the Latvian Relief Organization had resulted in
16,000 affidavits secured for Latvian displaced persons entering the U.S.A.

Members of the Latvian male double-quartet Tēvija (Fatherland) arrived in Boston together through a coordinated immigration, that forestalled dispersal of the artistic group.
This was musically one of the most imposing Latvian D.P.
choral groups, which had entertained American forces in
occupied Germany. Tēvija has continued to appear in concerts in the U.S.A., and published recorded performances.

Eduards Stukelis (1884-1956), a priest, became a represen-
tative of Latvian Catholics at the War Relief Service in New
York. He had been chancellor of the archdiocesis of Rīga
from 1924 to 1944. As representative of the archdiocesis,
Stukelis had participated in Catholic congresses in Chicago,
Oxford, Stockholm, and other major cities.

Jānis Garklāvs, an Orthodox bishop, came to the U.S.A.
and was appointed bishop of Detroit and Cleveland. Since
1950, he has held the post of assistant to the Metropolit of
of the U.S.A. Garklāvs had been appointed bishop of Rīga
in 1943.

1950   January 6. The American chapter of the Latvian Welfare
Organization Daugavas Vanagi (DV), was founded in New
York. Daugavas Vanagi originated in 1945 in western Germany and united Latvian war veterans then living in American, British, and French prison-of-war camps. Following
the emigration of its members, DV is now active in thirteen

countries.   Col. Vilis Janums was elected president
and led the organization from Germany for twenty-five years.
The largest memberships reside in the U.S.A., England,
Australia, Germany, and Canada. Of its roughly ten thousand members about three thousand live in the U.S.A. and
belong to one of its twenty-five local chapters. DV is mainly a welfare organization extending its support to war veterans and their families. It sponsors various fund-raising
cultural and social events, such as local choir concerts,
theater and folk-dance performances. DV publishes a bi-
weekly newspaper Latvija Amerika (Latvia in America), a
monthly magazine Daugavas Vanagi, a monthly bulletin,
song collections for male and female voices, books, records,
and other materials. DV is governed by annual congresses
of its members. Because of its strong nationalistic character and deep involvement in the Latvian cultural affairs in
the free world, DV is frequently attacked by the communist
press of Soviet-occupied Latvia.

The American Latvian Baptist Association (ALBA) was
founded by delegates from the Latvian Baptist parishes in
the U.S.A. It is registered with the American Baptist Convention and the Baptist World Alliance. ALBA also sponsors
several cultural activities. Most important are the Baptist
song days, where classical religious music and choral
works by Latvian composers are sung. Since 1950 nineteen
such song days have been held in various U.S. cities.

After a long hiatus, books in the Latvian language were published again in the U.S.A. About twenty-five titles appeared
in 1950.

Dace Epermanis, now a lawyer who has served as the district attorney of the State of New York, was the one hundred
and fifty thousandth displaced person to enter the United
States at the age of twelve.

The first one-man show by a Latvian painter for American
viewers was held by Ludolfs Liberts at the New York City
Library.

A number of Latvians volunteered for the Korean War. Several of them were killed in action. Pvt. Salinieks was
awarded the Distinguished Service Cross for extraordinary
heroism.

Maksimilians Mitrevics received the MacDowell Award for his painting Sunday at the National Academy of Design Annual in New York.

January 8. The first Latvian professional theater started its activities in New York with the comedy Ķīnas vāze (A Vase from China) by Mārtiņš Zīverts. Osvalds Uršteins directed the cast, which included Tonija Kalve, Hilda Prince, Ērika Šaumane, Ilga Blūmentāle, Juris Elksnītis, and Jēkabs Zaķis. The show was performed in Philadelphia on May 8 on the occasion of the fifty-eighth anniversary of the Philadelphia Society of Free Letts. Symbolically, this event represented a cultural meeting-point between two ideologically opposed generations of Latvian immigrants on American soil.

Latvian teenagers and students were organizing in youth groups in many U.S. cities, where DP's congregated. The Philadelphia youth group utilized the facilities of the Philadelphia Society of Free Letts to pursue a great variety of activities ranging from folk dancing to amateur film making. The youth group activities still take place at the Society of Free Letts in the 1970's.

Five Lutheran congregations organized by the earlier Latvian immigrants still existed: two in Boston, and one each in Philadelphia, Chicago, and New York. Three belonged to the Missouri Synod and two to the United Lutheran Church Association. Four of them owned their own church buildings. The first congregation to employ the newly arrived DP ministers were New York, Rev. Richards Zariņš, and Philadelphia, Rev. Jānis Siliņš.

1951

May. The Voice of America began its broadcasts in Latvian. These broadcasts are still continued. The Latvian Service employs a staff of nine persons and sends a total of two half-hour broadcasts daily. Information for these programs is derived from new agencies and a network of correspondents throughout the world. The Voice of America is a part of the U.S. Information Agency; its mission is to provide unbiased information and news for audiences in countries behind the Iron Curtain as well as for those in the free world.

The American Latvian Association in the United States was

founded in Washington, D.C. by 115 delegates from various
Latvian communities throughout the U.S.A. It coordinated
the social and cultural needs of the newly arrived immigrant group concerned with retaining its national identity.
This endeavor, encouraged by the Latvian legation, was espoused by 135 Latvian societies and religious congregations,
which recognized the need for a contralized organization to
represent their mutual interests.

The ALA is a non-profit, non-political organization, whose
officers and numerous volunteers serve without financial
reimbursement for personal time and services rendered.
It has had three presidents: from 1951 to 1970, Prof. Peter
P. Lejins; from 1970 to 1972, Uldis Grava, presently chairman of the Board of the World Federation of Free Latvians;
and from 1972, Dr. Ilgvars J. Spilners.

The ALA's activities are directed toward preserving the national identity of Latvians in America and toward advancing
recognition for the Latvian ethnic unity as an integral part
of modern American pluralism. Five bureaus, each devoted to a specific aspect of bicultural concerns, function
within the ALA:
  1) The Bureau of Education sponsors preparation of text-
books and related learning materials suitable for teaching
the Latvian language and other subjects in Latvian supplementary schools. Over two thousand children of American
Latvian families attend such supplementary schools and follow an elementary program for which general guidelines are
specified by ALA. To encourage bicultural studies, ALA
holds annual competitive examinations on a national level.
Students receiving the highest grades receive token mone-
tary awards as well as recognition in the Latvian press.
Furthermore, the Bureau of Education is also gradually
evolving a program of Latvian studies at higher educational
levels. Under its initiative and administration, a summer
high school, Beverīna, began its operations in Bucks County,
Pennsylvania on July 8, 1973. The college program at Western Michigan University receives publicity assistance as
well as some scholarship and research grants from the
ALA. Generally, the ALA devotes about 35 percent of its
annual budget to educational projects. The Bureau of Education has been directed by Mārtiņš Celms, Jānis Blumbergs, Dr. Tālivaldis Bērziņš, and Prof. Uldis Inveiss.
  2) The Bureau of Culture stimulates creative artistic pur-

suits in the Latvian communities, e.g. folk song and dance
festivals on a national level as well as locally. Art exhibits, folk-craft displays, concerts featuring Latvian composers and performers, lectures, discussion meetings, and
theater and film performances are also organized and supported. Many of these events involve intercontinental exchange of tours by prominent Latvian cultural personalities
in the free world. Two full-length documentary films on
the subject of Latvian activities in the free world have been
produced and shown to Latvian audiences in many countries.
Among other projects of cultural documentation is a series
of spoken recordings under the title Saule, saule, zeme,
zeme containing readings of excerpts from Latvian classical literature, which are rendered by notable Latvian stage
and screen performers. The directors of the Bureau of Culture have been Ēvalds Freivalds, Jānis Kadilis, Sr., Dr.
Pēteris Norvilis, Dr. Valda Melngaile, Dr. Visvaldis Klīve,
and Marģers Grīns.

 3) The Bureau of Sports coordinates inter-Latvian and in-
ter-Baltic championships in a number of sports activities,
such as basketball, table tennis, soccer, fencing, swim-
ming, skiing, tennis, track and field, and men's and women's volleyball. Latvian teams from various parts of the
U.S.A. have been competing formally with each other every
year since 1952. Many current players are the sons and
daughters of original team members. The ALA shares the
responsibility for organizing chess tournaments with the
Latvian Chess Association. Of documentary interest is
Latvijas sporta vēsture (History of Latvian Sports) by Vilis
Čika and Gunārs Gubiņš, published by the Bureau of Sports
in 1970, and a film about Latvian sports activities produced
in 1948. The Bureau of Sports has been directed by Vilis
Vuškalns, Arvīds Zāģeris, Jānis Robiņš and Teodors Ald-
zeris.

 4) The Bureau of Information commissions studies of the
present Soviet occupation in Latvia and its effect upon the
Latvian people. Relevant studies are used to inform the
American public about the processes of russification, religious oppression, and ethnic domination against the people
of Latvia who desire freedom and self-determination. This
bureau also supervises other public relations matters in
which the Latvian community seeks to identifiably assert
itself within the American community. The directors of the
Bureau of Information have been Alfrēds Bērziņš, Pēteris
Eglītis, Ilmārs Bergmanis, Norberts Trepša, Sigurds Rudzītis, Dr. Dzintars Paegle, Dr. Ilgvars Spilners, and Dr.
Tālivaldis Šmits.

5) The Bureau of Welfare has a predominantly informative function. Data are gathered and translated, advising individuals of Latvian descent of available federal and state welfare support in the U.S.A. The Bureau of Welfare has been directed by Harijs Lielnors, Arvīds Līdacis, Ludvigs Bērziņš, Andris Ritums, Arturs Valters, and is presently directed by Ingrīda Stravinskis.

A special feature of the ALA has been the Cultural Foundation, which has annually bestowed honorary awards to a number of persons and institutions of various professional fields for their outstanding achievements in either promoting Latvian culture, or in advancing international scientific knowledge. Since January 1, 1973, the functions of the Cultural Foundation of the ALA have been delegated to the Cultural Foundation of the World Federation of Free Latvians, of which the ALA is a member organization. In this capacity, the ALA shares its obligations with other participating Latvian central organizations in Australia and New Zealand, Canada, Western Europe, and South America.

The ALA is also a member of the Joint Baltic American Committee, where contact is maintained with related Lithuanian and Estonian cultural organizations. The ALA's informational activities in the World Federation of Free Latvians are managed, however, by the Bureau of Information. An annual congress of delegates elects sixteen officers to the Executive Board of Directors, who may reside in any part of the U.S.A. Individual bureaus are operated from diverse geographic locations. The association maintains a center administrative office in Washington, D.C., managed by Secretary General Bruno Albāts, who has served in his post since 1951.

The Latvian theater in the U.S.A. is dominated by renowned stage personalities from the major theaters of independent Latvia, and assisted by a select group of younger actors trained in exile. The American Latvian Theater, Boston Ensemble, was founded in Boston by Reinis Birzgalis. His ensemble usually presents monumental, historically oriented works of the classic Latvian drama. The first production of the Boston Ensemble was No saldenās pudeles (From the Bottle of Sweet Wine) by Rūdolfs Blaumanis. It had five performances in Boston, Philadelphia, and New York. Professional actors of the Latvian stage of Boston include Ance Rozīte, Valfrīds Streips, Kārlis Veics, and Jānis Lejiņš. A younger generation of emerging actors in Boston include Rasma Birzgalis, the founder's daughter; Vitolds Vītols, Lolita Lejiņa, Gunārs Straumēns, Silvestrs and Valentīna Lambergs.

In July the Committee for a Free Europe was founded as a
vehicle through which the former statesmen and political
leaders of nine East European captive nations (Latvia, Estonia, Lithuania, Poland, Czechoslovakia, Rumania, Bulgaria, Hungary and Albania) would work toward the liberation of their communist-occupied countries and aid their
exiles abroad. The Latvian section, later the Committee
for a Free Latvia, was directed by Vilis Māsēns. A Baltic
Freedom Council was formed within the same framework,
representing the Committee for a Free Latvia, Lithuania
and Estonia.

Latvian scouting in New York commemorated its second
anniversary since the registration of the first Latvian group
of Rowers Rīga with the Boy Scouts of America and that of
Zilais kalns with the Girl Scouts of America in 1949. In
two years the composite membership of both units at all levels had grown to 140 in the New York City area. They
formed a folk-dance group Trejdeksnis, and have been decorated for various activities in competition with American
scout units. Latvian scouting units are active in other Latvian communities, particularly in Cleveland, Kalamazoo,
and Chicago. New York leaders of Girl Scouts and Boy
Scouts are Mr. and Mrs. Gaujenieks, who founded the units
and are still in charge in 1973. National leaders of the Latvian scout movement are Elizabete Laufers, Vilhelmine
Vilks, and Fricis Sīpols.

The legation of Latvia acquired its permanent quarters at
17th and Webster Streets, N.W., Washington, D.C.

March 10. The first large-scale Latvian concert was organized at the Academy of Music in Brooklyn, New York.

Latvian astronomer Valfrīds Osvalds came to the U.S.A.
and became an assistant astronomer at the McCormick Ob-
servatory in Charlottesville, Virginia. Since 1957 he has
been an astronomer at the University of Virginia Observa-
tory, where he became professor emeritus in 1961. Osvalds
has published numerous scientific articles in English and
German; he is a member of the American Society of Astronomers, as well as several international professional societies of astronomers.

Richard Hansen-Liepiņš died. He had fled to Boston from
Latvia in 1905, because the Czarist regime was about to de-

port him to Siberia. From 1917, Hansen-Liepiņš was the
ideologist of the leftist Latvian press in the U.S.A.

1952   The Latvian Relief Fund of America was founded in Pennsylvania and is financially the best established Latvian organization in the U.S.A. It was designed to provide the state's
immigrant Latvians with the security of a minimal life insurance plan through a mutual assistance foundation. The
fund gradually expanded its membership and diversified its
functions. By 1972 its twelve thousand members of Latvian
descent from the fifty States and Canada were subscribing
to a wide variety of life, hospitalization, disability and un-
employment insurance programs.

Ideologically, the Latvian Relief Fund of America relied
upon a premise basic to the entire post-World War II immigration of Latvians. Only the able-bodied, employable refugees were admitted. It was explicitly understood that they
were not to burden the U.S. public welfare and relief programs, but were to seek immediate economic self-suffici-
ency within the general work force. The American free en-
terprise system presupposes private insurance against illness or death. To the economically insecure immigrants
this approach represented an ominous threat. The fund rose
to provide security adapted to the insurance needs and financial capabilities of its immigrant members; the fund also
maintained the Latvians' self-respect by insuring their self-
sufficiency in America.

The services of the fund expanded along with the growing
prosperity of its constituents. Unlike commercial insurance
companies, the Latvian Relief Fund of America is a non-
profit organization governed by its members through the
democratic process. An annual congress of elected delegates from the entire membership votes for a borad of executives and an auditing committee. Resolutions and policies established by this congress are binding to all members.
Administrative offices of the fund are located in Elkins Park,
Pennsylvania. Mr. Ludvigs Bērziņš has served as the executive president of the fund since its foundation. Rev. A.
Reinsons and A. Rudzis served on the first board of executives and have remained in office ever since.

In addition to its insurance services, the fund also provides a number of welfare services. In special cases, insurance dues may be waived for poverty-stricken members,
while their eligibility for benefits remains in force. A special fund exists to aid members who have exhausted their
insurance provisions and remain in need. The fund also

makes special admission arrangements for elderly Latvians,
whose age renders them ineligible for insurance in commercial establishments. Upon the birth of a child, a member
family receives a sum of $50.00 as a maternity gift, in ad-
dition to their hospitalization insurance benefits. In addition, several important building projects of Latvian churches
and community centers have been financed by the fund on
advantageous terms. Over $35,000.00 of the fund's re-
sources have been donated to support a wide variety of special causes for the enhancement of Latvian cultural life in
America.

The American Latvian Youth Association was founded under
the sponsorship of the American Latvian Association. Its
first president was Kristaps Valters, Jr. The purpose of
the association was to unite the Latvian-American youth and
advance youth activities in local Latvian communities
throughout the U.S.A. Over the years the scope of its activities has increased, especially after the general awakening of ethnic interest in the U.S.A. The association has
sponsored a number of projects, including ethnic heritage
seminars for Latvian youth groups. With the increasing af-
fluence of the Latvian communities in the U.S.A., the members of the association have been able to internationalize
their activities and to meet with Latvians of their own generation from other parts of the free world. The American
Latvian Youth Association actively participated in organizing two Latvian World Youth Congresses, one in Hanover
and Berlin, West Germany in 1970, and one in London, England in 1972. Andrejs Smiltārs presided over the organization in 1973.

The American National Latvian League in Boston purchased
its present home in Jamaica Plain, Massachusetts.

A survey, conducted this year on the distribution of faculty
members of the University of Latvia, indicates the following: of 446 faculty members of 1939, 360 were abroad in
1952. Of these, 186 were living in the U.S.A., 54 in Sweden, 30 in Canada, 14 in Great Britain, and 11 in South
America (Source: P. Starcs. "L.U. attīstība un panākumi"
(The Development and Achievements of the University of
Latvia). Vārti (Gate), 1952, No. 1.)

Harijs Lielnors (born in 1900 in Latvia), having managed
the Latvian section of the Voice of America for one year,
was advanced to special assistant of the European division.

Lielnors had arrived in the U.S.A. in 1923, and was instrumental in setting up the Latvian Relief Organization after
World War II.

The Latvian Press Association in the U.S.A. was founded.
The first president of this organization was Oļģerts Liepiņš,
followed by Jānis Porietis, Ēriks Raisters, and presently,
Viktors Irbe.

From 1952 to 1971 Latvians were well represented in the
Massachusetts fishing industry. In New Bedford in the
1960's, eight deep-sea fishing trawlers were Latvian-owned;
about one hundred Latvians worked as crewmen. Among
the boat owners were Bruno Štāls, Andrejs Pubalis, Runcis,
Kļaviņš and Trusis. By 1971 R. Brieže was the sole remaining entrepreneur with his trawlers Arianda and Hercules,
manned partially by a Latvian crew and the Skipper Jēkabs
Sniķeris.

1953   Viktors Vīksniņš (born 1923 in Latvia) was elected president
of the Chicago Latvian Association, and has continued in this
post to the present. He is also the founder and sole chairman to date of the Latvian Associations' Coordinating Center.
Likewise, he is very active in the captive nations' affairs in
Chicago.

WOJO, FM 105, of Evanston, Illinois began broadcasting a
weekly half-hour Latvian language program. For over
twenty years the broadcast has continued, presenting Latvian music and news and a monthly religious program.

August 16. Jules Feldmans, charge d'affaires of Latvia
serving at the legation of Latvia in Washington, D.C., died.

The Latvian Greek-Orthodox Synod in exile resumed its operations in the United States under the leadership of Metropolit Augustīns (died in 1959), with its headquarters in New
York City. It derived its jurisdiction over Latvians of that
faith from the patriarch of the Church of Constantinopolis.
There is also a Greek-Orthodox group in Philadelphia, Pennsylvania. Since 1959, the Synod has been headed by Archbishop Jānis in Chicago.

The first Latvian Song Festival in the United States was held
in Chicago, Illinois, in which nine hundred singers participated. It was estimated that every sixth Latvian in the
U.S.A. attended this festival either as a participant in the

program or as a spectator. The concert program of twenty-
one songs by Latvian composers was conducted by Valdemārs Ozoliņš, Bruno Skulte, Eduards Ramāts and Arnolds
Kalnājs. Honorary conductors were Ādolfs Ābele, formerly
dean of the Conservatory of Latvia, and a guest from Canada, Ērika Freimane. Subsequently, such festivals would
take place regularly every five years.

The Kersten Commission of the U.S. House of Representatives investigated Soviet aggression in the Baltic states. A
number of individual Latvians and representatives of Latvian organizations testified along with witnesses of other
Baltic nationalities.

Through public donations by Latvian communities in the
U.S.A., the painting Towers of Rīga by Ludolfs Liberts
was presented to President Dwight D. Eisenhower. This
painting was placed in the White House Oval Office and was
seen by large television audiences during the president's
televised press conferences from this room.

The first Baltic Concert Association was founded in Indianapolis, Indiana, by the Latvians Voldemārs Meļķis (pianist)
and Viktors Ziedonis (violinist), and Estonian conductor E.
Kalaman. Its purpose was to assure an annual seasonal
concert series of high artistic quality on a subscription basis. Similar concert associations were soon operating in
other Latvian centers, such as New York City, Chicago,
and Philadelphia.

Raimonds Staprāns (1926-), a painter, received his B.F.A.
degree from the University of California at Berkeley. Staprāns' name has become well-known throughout American
art circles. A 1972 intention to have a one-man show in
Rīga, Latvia, however, was aborted by Soviet authorities.

Pauls Puzinas, another Latvian artist, received the first
prize at the All-City Art Show in Los Angeles, California
for his painting titled Refugee Mother.

Harijs Gricēvičs was awarded the Gimbel's Prize in a Philadelphia art competition on the theme Philadelphia Today.

1954   Dr. Arnolds Spekke, a historian and a diplomat, was trans-
               ferred from Rome, Italy to assume the leadership of the
               Latvian legation in Washington, D.C. as charge d'affaires,

representing the Republic of Latvia. He published numerous articles and books on Latvian history and its political developments in Latvian, Italian, English, French, and German languages.

The Assembly of Captive European Nations (ACEN) was founded in New York, with the Committee for a Free Latvia as its co-founder. Its purpose was to expand throughout the world the activities of the U.S.-based Committee for a Free Europe. ACEN met on the opening date of UN sessions demonstratively, to emphasize the exclusion of the nine captive nationalities behind the Iron Curtain from this international assembly. Among the Latvian leaders were Pēteris Eglītis, Arvīds Zāģeris, Dainis Rudzītis, Sigurds Rudzītis, Alfrēds Bērziņš, Ādolfs Klīve, and Vilis Māsēns.

The Latvian Press Association unveiled a plaque in Lincoln, Nebraska commemorating a graduate of the University of Nebraska - Dr. Kārlis Ulmanis, the fourth president of Latvia.

The Latvian Evangelical Lutheran Church of Massachusetts purchased a 360-acre property for recreational purposes, Piesaule in New Hampshire, where they have since built summer camp facilities for children. Architect Vitolds Vītols designed the chapel and other structures at this site.

The first American-Latvian nation-wide competition in men's and women's volleyball and men's basketball took place in Minneapolis, Minnesota. This event gained such popularity that it has subsequently become an annual event hosted by different Latvian communities throughout the eastern and central states of the U.S.A.

The U.S. Congress adopted a measure permitting citizens of Latvia and the two other Baltic states of Estonia and Lithuania to hold U.S. federal government appointments.

Chess World, a Latvian chess magazine, edited by Aleksandrs Liepnieks, began publication.

The World Junior Chess Championship was held in Antwerp, Belgium with twenty-four participants from twenty-three countries. While Boris Spasky (USSR) won, Edmārs Mednis of New York, a Latvian representing the United States, took second place without a single loss.

The tenth U.S. Junior Chess Championship was held in Lincoln, Nebraska, with twenty-five participants, including the present world champion, Bobby Fisher. Latvian chess player Ivars Kalme from Philadelphia, won this tournament.

From 1954 to 1967 Olgerts Liepins published a Latvian newspaper, Amerikas Vēstnesis (American Herald) in Boston.

1955   November 18. Latvian independence commemorative services were held in the auditorium of the Boston Boys' Latin School. The principal speaker at this event was Sen. John F. Kennedy, the future president of the United States.

The Midwest Regional Latvian Song Festival was held in Milwaukee, Wisconsin, which presented 360 singers to an audience of about 4,000. The main concert was conducted by Pēteris Banders, Valdemārs Ozoliņš, and Eduards Ramats. The honorary conductor was Ernests Brusubārda, Sr., of Milwaukee, Wisconsin.

October 30. The Latvian Evangelical Lutheran Church of Seattle held the first service in their own chapel. Organized in 1950, the congregation was led from 1953 to 1963 by Prof. Kārlis Kundziņš, the foremost Latvian Lutheran theologian in America. The Seattle community, the Latvian Society of Washington State, and the Evangelical Lutheran congregation jointly purchased, remodeled, administered and used the Latvian building on Densmon Avenue North. It consisted of a social hall and religious chapel. The city of Seattle confiscated this building in 1970, converting the area into a recreational park site. The Latvians of Seattle subsequently erected an impressive new cultural center, combining chapel, school and social facilities.

The Kalamazoo Latvian Society purchased its own building.

Norma Elizabete Auziņa, violinist, graduated from the Julliard School of Music in New York with an M.S. degree. She toured the U.S.A. under the sponsorship of the Young Artists of American in 1957. She is the wife of American cellist Ronald Leonard, is on the faculty of the University of Rochester, Eastman School of Music, and is a violinist with the Rochester Symphony Orchestra.

David Fetler received a degree in music from the Eastman School of Music, and is on the faculty of the same institution, where he directs the Eastman Collegium Singers and Ensemble.

1956   The New York Latvian Evangelical Lutheran Church purchased a camp site in Elka Park, New York; it has since become a major summer camp center not only for Latvian children of the eastern United States, but also for children from Canada and South America. The use of the Latvian language in all activities is stressed.

The Latvian War Veterans Association (Daugavas Vanagi), Boston chapter, purchased a building formerly owned by a group of older Latvian immigrants to the U.S.A. The association took over and expanded a library of four thousand books that is housed there, which represents the largest collection of Latvian publications in the Free World. It is frequented by scholars and students alike for research purposes.

Aleksandrs Lauberts (born in 1908) and Osvalds Uršteins (born in 1910) directed the Voice of America broadcasts in Latvian from Germany, Munich Radio Center, until 1958. Lauberts was the Latvian correspondent for the United Press. He came to the U.S.A. in 1947, and started working for the U.S. Department of State in 1952. Uršteins is a prominent actor and director of the Latvian theater.

Silvestrs Lambergs broadcasted a thirty minute Latvian program on WBOS on Sundays in Boston. Political commentary on the show was done by Valdemars Lambergs, his father, who died in 1973.

Arved Brachman (1900-1956) died in Boston. He had played contrabass with the Boston Pops and St. Louis Symphony.

Paul Fetler received a Ph.D. from the University of Minnesota for his dissertation Symphony No. 3; he is a composer and a conductor of symphony orchestras.

Aleksandrs Liepnieks, editor of the Latvian chess magazine, Chess World, won the U.S. midwest championship in chess.

Edmãrs Mednis won the U.S. intercollegiate chess championship. He repeated his victory again in 1957.

1957

October 7. The Federation of Latvian Evangelical Lutheran Churches in America, Inc. (LELDAA) was founded as the central organization of the numerous Latvian Evangelical Lutheran congregations. Its three U.S. districts are headed by district deans of the Latvian Evangelical Lutheran Church in Exile, who are assisted by clergymen as well as laymen. The LELDAA functions as a member of the global Latvian Lutheran Church in Exile; it also publishes a regular magazine Ceļa Biedrs (Companion), provides the Latvian weekend supplementary schools with religious instructions, and organizes religious activities for Latvian Lutheran youth groups. The first president of the LELDAA was Prof. Kārlis Kundziņš; he was succeeded by Dean Aleksandrs Veinbergs, the pastor of the Latvian Evangelical Lutheran Church of Washington, D.C. and vicinity.

The Latvian Trio, consisting of Valdemārs Melķis (pianist), Jānis Ādamsons (cellist), and Viktors Ziedonis (violinist) toured the midwestern and western U.S.A., performing concerts for Latvian and American audiences. This chamber group was founded in 1945 in Augsburg, Germany. Since 1950 it has been based in Indianapolis, Indiana, where its leader, Viktors Ziedonis, settled. The trio has played in West Germany, Austria, the U.S.A. and Canada, receiving favorable reviews in the U.S. press, including the periodical Musical America. Other Latvian musicians who have played in the trio are Dzidris Treimanis, Ingus Nāruns, Eižens Freimanis, Vilma Delle-Grāvīte, V. Heckmanis and Verēna Stelpe-Dambrāne.

Adele Pulciņa-Karpa (1902-1957), an opera singer, died. She had studied at the Latvian Conservatory of Music in Paris. She had been a lyric soprano at the Latvian National Opera in Riga from 1925 to 1932, and from 1936 to 1944, and on the faculty of the conservatory from 1941 to 1944. While in the United States, she taught singing at the Wisconsin Conservatory in Milwaukee from 1952 to 1957. She was the wife of Dr. Ansis Karps.

1958

July 5. The second Latvian Song Festival in the U.S.A. was held in New York City, with 38 choirs and 900 singers participating in the program, and about 10,000 in the audience. The grand concert was conducted by Ādolfs Ābele, Bruno Skulte, and Arnolds Kalnājs. In addition to the main event, there were several other notable activities, including a special concert performing new compositions; an art ex-

hibit of 278 works by 94 participating painters from 11 countries; an exhibit of arts and crafts, and several conferences
by the members of the American Latvian Association and
various other professional and social organizations. This
second song festival received a wide publicity in Latvian as
well as in the American press.

The Latvian Youth Publishing Society, Ceļinieks (Wayfarer)
was founded. It publishes the Latvian literary magazine
Jaunā Gaita (The New Path), and the Latvian children's magazine Mazputniņš (The Little Bird), as well as books in the
Latvian language.

August 9. The first nationwide track and field competition
of Latvian athletes was held in Indianapolis, Indiana.

The Latvian Society of Chicago, Illinois, purchased its own
building.

Ludolfs Liberts, one of the best known Latvian artists, died
in New York.

Painter Nora Drapče received an honorary award and a mon-
etary stipend from the Kalamazoo, Michigan Civic Fund for
her efforts to activate and popularize the fine arts in the
Kalamazoo locality.

Ingrīda Gutberga-Johansen earned the Mus. A.D. for her
dissertation Evolution of the Piano Quartet and Piano Quin-
tet to the End of the Nineteenth Century at Boston University.

Karina Gutberga-Davis earned her Mus. A.D. degree at
Boston University for the dissertation Keyboard Music for
Two Performers from the Early Beginnings to the Middle of
the Nineteenth Century. These two Latvian-born sisters
are duo-pianists, who have performed across the U.S.A.
Both are 1950 graduates of the Mozarteum in Salzburg, Austria. Both are on the faculty of Boston University.

Anda Ūdris-Andersons was selected by the U.S. Department
of State as one of 165 American students to serve as guides
at the American pavillion of the Brussels World's Fair in
Belgium.

1959   Mazputniņš is an international monthly magazine for Latvian
                children edited by Laimonis and Līga Streips in Chicago,

Illinois. Besides a regular staff, it draws upon numerous contributing authors and illustrators of professional rank, who have endowed this publication with artistic and educational quality. This project, now in its fourteenth year, is among the most important American-based cultural services that benefit the international Latvian community.

The first Latvian Youth Festival was held in Toronto, Canada, with a heavy participation of Latvian youth from the U.S.A.

St. John's Latvian Evangelical Lutheran Church of Chicago, Illinois, purchased its own church building.

The Latvian Heritage Foundation in Boston arranged an English language series of broadcasts designed to introduce Americans to Latvian music, art and literature. Aired over WCRB in Boston, the half-hour programs are directed by Silvestrs Lambergs and were still on the air in 1973.

Jānis Rīsbergs (1918 -) gained controlling interest and became the president of General Builders Corporation, the only Latvian-controlled business listed on a major stock-exchange. Rīsbergs had started in 1949 as a contractor for Levitt, evolving his own business through a series of daring ventures that earned him the title of "Crazy Latvian." General Builders constructs single homes and condominiums in New York and Florida. Among its construction workers more than one thousand are Latvians. General Builders employs another one thousand Latvians through sub-contractors, and at least some one hundred of its professional engineers, technical and administrative personnel are of Latvian origin.

Painter Svens Lūkins from New York made his first "shaped canvas." Mr. Lūkins pioneered this new direction in painting, which is considered one of the major innovations in modern American art.

Jānis Annuss received the Prix de Rome (Edwin Austin Abbey Memorial Fellowship) for studies at the American Academy in Rome. This grant was renewed for 1960.

George J. Longworth, an historian and instructor in political science at Columbia University, and since 1961 at the University of South Carolina, published The Latvian Congress of Rural Delegates in 1905, an historical study.

Jānis Kļaviņš graduated from the Schleswig-Holstein Academy of Music in Germany cum laude; in the same year, he received a Dr. Med. degree from the University of Kiel, Germany. Kļaviņš is presently on the faculty of New York state and Long Island universities, and the director of the pathology division of the Brooklyn-Cumberland Medical Center. He is the author of some ninety scientific publications. Dr. Kļaviņš can frequently be heard as a soloist (baritone) in independent concerts in New York and at Latvian commemorative events as well. In 1972, Dr. Kļaviņš was hailed for a major advance in cancer research proving the primitive similarity of embryonic and cancer cells, both of which lack specialization.

Leonids Dreibergs from Saginaw, Michigan, was placed as the best correspondence chess player in the U.S.A.

1960   A study sponsored by the American Latvian Association shows that about 400 Latvian organizations and congregations exist in some 60-70 localities in the U.S.A. In eight such centers Councils of Latvian Organizations have been established to better coordinate the diverse activities of Latvian organizations and sponsor major common events.

Congregations: A total of 100 congregations existed.

Religious Affiliation	Total No. of Congregations	No. of Locations
Lutheran	80	59
Roman Catholic	12	12
Baptist	6	6
Orthodox	2	2
Total:	100	

Most of the congregations were founded around 1950 following the influx of Latvians under the Displaced Persons Act. The largest Lutheran congregation is in New York with 3,635 registered members; 13 others have memberships of more than 400, while the size of the majority of congregations is below 250. Most Lutheran congregations are unified under the Federation of Latvian Evangelical Lutheran Church in America (LELDAA). The American Latvian Catholic Association coordinates the 12 Roman Catholic congregations of which the Indianapolis congregation is the largest with 340 members. The American Latvian Baptist Association unifies the Baptists.

Latvian societies, existing in 43 locations, usually play the leading role in Latvian community activities. Four of these societies had been founded prior to the end of World War II (Philadelphia, 1892; New York, 1892; Boston, 1917; Chicago, 1922), but most have been established since 1950. In 9 localities the membership of the society exceeds 200; the largest one is in the state of Washington with 430 members.

The Latvian Welfare Organization, Daugavas Vanagi, exists in 20 localities, with a total membership of 8,500. During the 10 years ending in 1959, Daugavas Vanagi collected almost $200,000. for welfare purposes. Other organizations, which include cultural (choirs, theater groups), professional (Latvian Doctors and Dentists Association, Association of Latvian Engineers, etc.), Latvian sports clubs, youth and student organizations are found in many Latvian localities. The largest Latvian organization is the American Latvian Association in the United States with over 8,000 members.

July 3. The Regional Midwest Latvian Song Festival was held in Indianapolis, Indiana, with 24 choirs, 600 singers performing in the program, and about 5,500 people in the audience. The grand choir was conducted by Valdemārs Ozoliņš, Valdemārs Meļķis, and Arnolds Kalnājs. Two cantatas sung by the choir were on a festival program for the first time: Trauksme 18. novembra naktī by Arnolds Kalnājs, and Aglonas Dievmātei by Jānis Mediņš. Symphonic music appeared for the first time on the program of a Latvian festival in the U.S.A. when Symphony No. 1 by Tālivaldis Ķeniņš and Suite for Flute and Orchestra by Arnolds Šturms were premiered at this event. A. Šturms performed the solo for his own composition.

Dr. Edgar Andersons, professor of history at San Jose State University, California, led an international archaeological and historical expedition to the West Indies. He found many traces of early Latvian settlements on the Island of Tobago.

July 12. At the Biltmore Hotel in Los Angeles, Democratic presidential candidate John F. Kennedy met with a delegate from the American Latvian Association, Mr. Helmūts Braukis. Latvian suggestions for the party platform on foreign

policy had been entered on the agenda and accepted by the
Democratic Convention.

The first Latvian credit union in the U.S.A. was founded
in Cleveland, Ohio. Subsequently, several other such credit unions have been formed in various U.S. Latvian centers: Wisconsin, 1961; Illinois, 1963; Detroit, Michigan,
1963; Grand Rapids, Michigan, 1964.

A theater ensemble was formed by professional actors from
the two major theaters of independent Latvia, now residing
in New York and Washington, D.C. areas. This ensemble
has specialized in modern Latvian comedy. Besides other
repertoire, they render polished stage adaptations of the
California novelist Anšlavs Eglītis' social satires. The ensemble is directed by Osvalds Uršteins, who is effectively
supported by Hilda Prince and Anda Uršteins, the director's
wife and daughter respectively. Other actors of the younger
generation have been trained by Mr. Uršteins -- notably
Vilnis Baumanis of New York and Maija Lelis of Washington,
D.C.

The American Latvian Theatre, Boston Ensemble, performed Skabarga sirdī (A Wounded Heart) by Jānis Lejiņš.

The Bucks County Latvian Baptist Community in Pennsylvania purchased a seventeen-acre property for recreational
purposes. Camp facilities were developed on the site and
summer programs are held for Latvian children. This later became the location of the East Coast Latvian summer
high-school Beverīna, launched in 1973 under the leadership
of A. Liepkalns of Boston.

The popular musical-satyrical group, Čikagas Piecīši, was
founded under the leadership of Alberts Legzdiņš.

At the Chess Olympiad in Leningrad, U.S.S.R., the U.S.
team, including two Latvians, Edmārs Mednis and Ivars
Kalme, won.

1961   April 27. On the initiative of the American Latvian Association, the Joint Baltic American Committee was founded
in Washington, D.C. Its membership includes the three
nationwide central Baltic organizations in the U.S.A.: the
Estonian American National Council, the American Latvian
Association in the United States, and the Lithuanian Ameri-

can Council. The purpose of this committee is to coordinate political activities of the three Baltic nationalities within the realm of U.S. foreign policy. This committee is presided in turn by member organizations.

Dr. Karlis Dravnieks, an engineer and a wood hobbyist in
Wisconsin, constructed an antiquated Latvian instrument,
the kokle, after authentic plans furnished by the ethnologist
Leonīds Linauts. The musicologist Andrejs Jansons used
this instrument to experiment with its musical potential and
to reconstruct its playing techniques. Additional woodcrafts-
men in the U.S.A. gradually familiarized themselves with
the construction of the kokle; by 1963 Jansons was able
to equip and organize the Latvian Folk Ensemble of New
York. This was the beginning of a unique cultural movement for Latvians in the U.S.A. that has enhanced the scope
of Latvian music. About one hundred arrangements and
original compositions have been writeen for the kokle within a decade. Quantities of little-known folk material have
been resurrected from archives and made popular by kokle
players.

The Latvian Welfare Association, Daugavas Vanagi of Des
Moines, Iowa, purchased a ten acre property for recreational facilities.

Four Latvian congregations purchased their own churches:
the Latvian Baptist Community in Philadelphia, Pennsylvania,
the Latvian Evangelical Lutheran Church of Martin Luther
of Fond du Lac, Wisconsin, St. John's Latvian Evangelical
Lutheran Church of Kalamazoo, Michigan, and the Latvian
Evangelical Lutheran Church of Grand Rapids, Michigan.

The American Latvian Theatre of Washington, D.C., toured
the U.S.A. with Omartija kundze (Mrs. Omartijs) by Anšlavs Eglītis. They gave a total of thirty-two performances
in their 1961 and 1962 tours.

The American Latvian Theatre, Boston Ensemble, performed Put, vejini (Blow, ye Winds) by Rainis in Boston,
New York, Toronto and Willimantic.

Leon "Jake" Swirbul, president of Grumman Aircraft, died.
Initially, Swirbul had worked as a foreman at Grumman
Aircraft during World War I. He was active in fund-raising
efforts for youth activities. He became a brigadier general

during World War II, and was in charge of air transport
services in the Pacific theater of war. To date he has been
the highest ranking Latvian in the U.S. armed forces.

A method for determining CO_2 content in coal and other
substances, developed by Pēteris Otto Krūmiņš (born in
1898 in Karzdaba, died in 1964 in Ohio), a Latvian chemical engineer, head of the Research Division for Solid and
Synthetic Fuels, College of Engineering at Ohio State University, was confirmed in the Book of ASTM Standards as
the official U.S. method. Krūmiņš is also the author of
more than thirty research publications, including the chapter on "Coal and Coke" in the 1963 sixth edition of Standard
Methods of Chemical Analysis, the authoritative textbook in
the field. Krūmiņš was the recipient of an honorary award
from the Latvian Cultural Foundation in 1964.

The Latvian Chess Club of Chicago, Illinois, won the city
championship against seven other teams. Jānis Tums became the chess champion of Chicago, Illinois, winning all
games of the annual tournament.

Vitauts Sīmanis, a painter, received the prize of the Alumni
Association of the Art Institute of Chicago for one of his
works.

1962   October 7. At the Latvian Evangelical Lutheran Church in
Hyattsville, Maryland, Kārlis Kundziņš, former professor
of Theology at the University of Latvia, pastor of the Latvian Evangelical Lutheran Church in Seattle, Washington,
was ordained archbishop of the Latvian Evangelical Lutheran
Church in exile with jurisdiction over Latvian Lutherans
throughout the free world. Kundziņš succeeded Archbishop
Teodors Grīnbergs, who had been elevated to the office in
1932 and had guided the church in exile from West Germany
since 1944.

June 23. The first Latvian Song Festival on the West Coast
was held in Seattle, Washington, featuring nine choirs with
201 singers. This festival was cosponsored by the Latvian
Society of Washington State and the School of Music of the
University of Washington. The grand choir was conducted
by Pēteris Galiņš, Arvīds Grants, and Valdemārs Ozoliņš.
Accompanying events were an art exhibit, a male choir concert, and a theater performance of Minhauzena precības
(Courtship of Muenchhausen) by Mārtiņš Zīverts with dramatists of Los Angeles directed by Vilis Lapenieks.

June 24. Volfgangs Dārziņš (born in 1906 in Latvia), a concert pianist, teacher, music critic, scholar and composer,
died in Seattle. Dārziņš' compositions were included in the
program of the Seattle song festival, and he had done much
to plan and promote this event. He was also on the faculty
of the School of Music at the University of Washington and
taught privately as well. Kenneth Benshoof, Myrtle Estelle,
and Andres Andreassen were among his students who have
interpreted and popularized Dārziņš' works. A commemorative fund was established in Dārziņš' name at the University of Washington.

Americans for Congressional Action to free the Baltic States
was founded. This was a lobbyist group whose efforts subsequently culminated in a passage of Congress-House Resolution No. 416 reaffirming the United States position on the
nonrecognition of the forcible incorporation of the Baltic
states of Estonia, Latvia and Lithuania into the Soviet Union.

The Second Youth Festival was held in Chicago, Illinois.
The idea of 2 x 2, a Latvian youth seminar, was conceived
in preparation for this event. The pilot program was limited, confined to the time-span and inner-city location of the
festival. The name of the project symbolizes its aims.
The 2 x 2 experience is designed to equip a young Latvian
with basic information and understanding of the Latvian ethnic community, and to help him toward a meaningful personal relationship to it. From this fundamental "multipli-
cation table" a young person should be able to evolve the
proper combination for his own identity, using the Latvian
heritage to enhance his role in the dominant American society. The 2 x 2 program has subsequently evolved into the
most respected and versatile program for young adults of
Latvian origin in America. It is sponsored by the Latvian
Youth Association of America.

A Latvian ethnographic section was opened at the Reading
Public Museum in Pennsylvania containing three permanent
exhibits. Exhibit I contains Latvian artifacts of the ninth
to sixteenth centuries: a complete twelfth century female
costume, reconstructed after an archaelogical original, re-
markable for a shawl decorated with 2728 separate brass
rings worked into the woven material. It also contains an
excellent collection of amber artifacts - one item dates
from 500 B.C., and a collection of brass and silver ornaments - bracelets, necklaces, etc. One of the ornaments,

an original recovered in 1935 from a lake bottom at Vilku muiža in Latvia, dates from the eleventh century. Exhibit II contains Latvian artifacts of the seventeenth through twentieth centuries including a complete nineteenth century female costume from the region of Nica. The silver ornaments are original, dating from 1792 and signed by the silversmith Juris Klīve. Two woven specimens of decorative shawls date from the 1790's. Exhibit III contains artifacts from the twentieth century including fine examples of modern jewelry design based on an ancient heritage of Latvian ornamentation and the art of wrought silver forging.

The American Latvian Association organized an exhibit of Latvian art at the Reading Museum of Art in Pennsylvania. Sixty-one artists with 196 individual works were represented.

A poetry anthology Dzejas un Sejas (Poems and Faces) was published by Grāmatu Draugs, presenting Latvian verse and its authors since 1950. This was an event in Latvian literature, for more than one half of the inclusions were devoted to the "younger generation" of poets, who started their careers in literature in exile and had been too young to publish their works in Latvia. Between seven and twelve new volumes of Latvian poetry appear outside of Latvia every year with a distribution of five hundred to one thousand copies each. Among the poets representing this new generation are Gunārs Saliņš, Olafs Stumbrs, Baiba Bičole, Astrīda Ivask, Rita Gāle, and Valda Melngaile.

A major Latvian Boy Scout and Girl Scout camp, Latvija, was held near Kalamazoo, Michigan.

The Latvian Evangelical Lutheran Church of Christ of Detroit, Michigan, purchased a building that the congregation later remodeled into a chapel.

Latvians in Denver, Colorado, celebrated the tenth anniversary of their amateur theater, which had regularly prepared one production a year since 1952.

Gundars Pone, a violinist, received a Ph.D. in music from the University of Minnesota. Pone is a composer, a member of the Webern International Society, and a professor at the New York College of Liberal Arts at the State University of New York at New Paltz. Pone's Quattro temperamenti

d'amore for orchestra received its premiere at New Paltz
in 1970 by the Buffalo Symphony Orchestra under the leadership of Lucas Foss. Pone also received a New York State
University commission to compose an opera based on a
documentary biography of Rosa Luxemburg. The libretto
is being written by another Latvian musician, Longins Apkalns.

Mārtiņš Šlessers, specialist in bird photography, was
awarded a Gold Medal by the Washington, D.C. Society of
Cinematographers for his film Bathing Habits of Song Birds.
Šlessers' articles on birds have appeared in Natural History magazine published by the American Museum of Natural History in New York.

Soil Mechanics, a definitive geotechnics text, was published.
It was authored by Alfrēds Richards Jumiķis, a professor
at Rutgers University. Jumiķis is the director of Rutger's
geotechnical laboratory, specializing in the effects of frost
upon highway engineering.

Historian Aleksandrs Berķis, Ph.D., was appointed professor at Longwood College, Virginia. Berķis has been an
active letter writer to the American press on the question
of communism.

Although nominally the World Federation of Free Latvians
(WFFL) had been founded in 1955, the first meeting of its
executive board was held in Washington, D.C., with delegates from the U.S.A., Canada, Europe and Australia.
The WFFL unites Latvian central organizations in the Free
World: the United States, Canada, Australia and New Zealand, South America and Western Europe. This organization attests to the unity of the Latvian nation and its inalien-
able rights to live in its land. It asserts the rights of Latvians in their homeland to freedom and self-determination,
and tries to unite Latvian activities in the free world toward
the re-establishment of a free and independent Latvia. Its
present headquarters is with the American Latvian Association in the U.S.A.

1963   September 1. The Third Latvian Song Festival in the United
            States was held in Cleveland, Ohio. Thirty-six choirs with
            950 singers participated in the program, attended by an es-
            timated 10,000 listeners. The grand choir was directed by
            Arnolds Kalnājs, Bruno Skulte, and Arvīds Purvs from To-

ronto, Canada. Among other notable events, there was also a concert program dedicated to the compositions of Jāzeps Vītols, attended by almost 2,000 people. Vītols' compositions were performed by Mirdza Grimma-Štrausa - soprano, Hugo Štrauss - pianist, Valdemars Ruševics - violinist, the mixed choir Dziesmu Vairogs conducted by Arnolds Kalnājs, and a specially organized string quartet.
Another outstanding event was the performance of Latvian
folk dances including 12 different dances, with participants
from Latvian youth groups from various Latvian centers in
the U.S.A. This performance turned out to be almost as
popular as the grand concert of choirs itself.

Latvian Day at the New York World's Fair was marked by
a program of ethnic songs and dances. A joint choir composed of eight East Coast Latvian choral groups of a total
of two hundred singers sang folk song arrangements under
the direction of Bruno Skulte. Five folk-dance groups performed ten Latvian folk dances to an accompaniment of an
instrumental ensemble of winds and strings including the
kokle, for which the music was especially arranged by Kārlis Lietiņš.

Technikas Apskats (Technical Review), issued four times
a year by the Latvian Association of Engineers Abroad (Latviešu Inženieru Apvienība Ārzemēs), marked a decade of
uninterrupted publication, surpassing in this respect all
other technical journals ever published in Latvian. It serves
and publishes articles by Latvian engineers, technical scientists and architects throughout the free world. It is edited by K. Ieleja, A. Spurmanis, with A. Kroms, M. Straumanis, J. Baumanis and M. Aserīte as the editorial consul-
tants. Its articles are abstracted by Chemical Abstracts
(Columbus, Ohio). Besides scientific articles on current
developments, the journal offers historical documentation
of technological achievements in independent Latvia and cul-
tivates the systematic expansion of technical terminology
in the Latvian language.

A 2 x 2 youth study camp was held in Michigan. The camp
has retained the same successful format every year since
1963. About one hundred select Latvians of college age
joined interest groups, and followed a week's intensive study
schedule in a secluded rural setting. Many prominent Latvians, experts in their professional fields, participated as
guest lecturers. The program was divided into three ma-

jor interest groups: history and politics, literature, and
folklore. Subsequent programs have offered other choices,
such as dramatics, music, Latvian language, and education. This camp was led by Brunis Rubess, a long-time
Scout master and an experienced youth leader.

Linards Tauns (born in 1922 in Latvia), a gifted and innovative poet, died tragically in New York. Tauns was a poet
of the city; his themes superimposed the old world upon the
new and represented a new direction of Latvian poetry. Until his death, he had published two volumes of poetry. A
third was issued posthumously in 1972.

The American Latvian Theatre of Washington, D.C. toured
U.S. Latvian communities, performing Vilks Rīgā (The
Wolf of Riga) by Teodors Zeltiņš, giving a total of nineteen
performances.

The West Coast Latvian Theater under the direction of Vilis Lapenieks in Los Angeles started with a production of
Lapenieks' Iebūvieša liksta (Settler's Troubles). They
also performed a concert version of Jāzeps un viņa brāli
(Joseph and his Brothers) by Rainis in a church setting.
The role of Joseph was played by Olafs Stumbrs, known
as a poet.

The Pacific Palisades Latvian Dramatists had the first of
their "coast to coast" theater tours, visiting thirty U.S.
Latvian centers with their productions of Cilvēks grib spē-
lēt (Man wants to play) by Anšlavs Eglītis, directed by Ansis Tipāns with decorations by Veronika Janelsiņa (in private life Mrs. Anšlavs Eglītis), starring M. Cukura, Spodra Zaļuma and Ansis Tipāns. This production was awarded the citation for 1963 by the American Latvian Association Cultural Foundation.

The American Latvian Theatre, Boston Ensemble, performed Intermecco Ilguciemā (Intermezzo in the village)
by U. Siliņš in Boston, Toronto, Willimantic, New York
and Washington, D.C.

The Latvian Society of Grand Rapids, Michigan, built its
own building.

The Latvian Evangelical Lutheran Church of Grand Rapids,
Michigan, purchased a property of eighty acres.

Jacob Sieberg, the founder of the American National Latvian League, died in Boston at the age of one hundred.

Mārīte Ozers of Chicago, Illinois, was selected Miss U.S.A.. This may have been the first time that a foreign-born girl represented the United States in the world-wide Miss Universe beauty contest.

Juris Upatnieks, working at the University of Michigan in Ann Arbor, co-invented holography, a form of direct photography using laser beams and eliminating the negative stage of an image.

Ivars Hiršs, son of Roberts Hiršs, received the Helen Critchet Award for his show at the Triangle Gallery of San Francisco, California. He also held a one-man show at the Pratt Graphic Arts Center in New York, and has regularly exhibited his paintings at the Gump's art salon, San Francisco, since 1965. His works have also been exhibited at the Smithsonian Institution and the White House in Washington, D.C., and at the Legion of Honour and San Francisco Museum of Art.

Elmārs Ezeriņš played at the Rose Bowl on the University of Wisconsin football team.

The Journalism School at Columbia University gave the Berger Prize to Peter Kihss , a member of the New York Times editorial staff.

Juris Zvērs won the Bell System Correspondence Chess Tournament against 783 participants without a single loss.

1964   The thirteenth annual Congress of the American Latvian Association was held in Boston, Massachusetts, with 101 participating delegates. On this occasion, John Collins, the mayor of Boston, proclaimed May 1 as Latvian Day, and the red-white-red flag of Latvia was raised over the city hall of Boston.

November 17. Dr. Vilis Māsēns (born in 1902 in Latvia) died in New York. A graduate of the University of Latvia, Māsēns earned a Dr. iur. summa cum laude at the University of Heidelberg, Germany, and specialized further in international relations in London and Paris. From 1936 to 1940 he led the Baltic desk at the foreign ministry of Latvia.

In post-World War II Germany he was associated with the
Latvian Central Committee International Relief Organization.
In New York since 1951, Māsēns chaired the Committee for
Free Latvia.

Under the direction of Ansis Tipāns, a production of Kur-
purū by Mārtiņš Zīverts was staged in Los Angeles. Members of the cast were Spodra Zaļuma, Maruta Ludeka, Ansis Tipāns, Olafs Stumbrs. Stage decorations were designed
by I. Tilgass. Thirty performances at Latvian communities throughout the continent were given.

Pacific Palisades Latvian Dramatists staged Ferdinands un
Sibilla (Ferdinand and Sybil) under the direction of the author, Anšlavs Eglītis, with stage decorations by Veronika
Janelsiņa, and actors M. Cukura, V. Toma, Māris Ubāns
and J. Ērglis. This production toured the entire U.S.A.,
visiting twenty-nine Latvian communities.

The American Latvian Theater of Washington, D.C., gave
two performances of Vilkate (Werewolf) by Aina Nebois.

The Latvian Folk Ensemble of New York gave its first performance at the New York World's Fair. The Latvian kokle
was heard for the first time by an American audience.

April 13. Dr. Natalija Mūrnieks (born in 1919 in Latvia), a
specialist in anesthesiology and rehabilitation medicine, was
one of the outstanding women scientists in the U.S.A. to be
honored at a special White House reception by President
Lyndon B. Johnson. Only two women from each state received this honor. Presently, Dr. Mūrnieks is with the
Veterans Administration Hospital, Danville, Illinois.

Eižens Dzelzkalējs, Latvian numismatist, received the first
prize at the New England American Numismatic Society exhibit in Boston.

Pauls Puzinas received the Andrew Carnegie Award at the
National Academy of Design Annual in New York.

Mārtiņš Šlessers received the second prize for a film titled
Taming of Song Birds from the Washington Society of Cinematographers in Washington, D.C.

Andris Staklis became the Midwest Students' Chess Champion.

1965   July 4. The second song festival of the West Coast was held
              in Portland, Oregon, with 13 choirs and 275 participating
              singers. Gov. M.O. Hatfield declared the first week in
              July Baltic Days. The series of Latvian events included art
              and craft exhibits, a religious concert, a special memorial
              concert dedicated to composer and pianist Volfgangs Dār-
              ziņš, a theater production of Jaunās asinis (The New Gene-
              ration) by Seattle's dramatists to commemorate the author,
              Valdemārs Kārkliņš, who died in 1964 in Oregon, and a
              folk-dance performance. At the grand festival concert, an
              audience of 4,000 heard 275 singers perform 20 choral
              works under the direction of Arvīds Berkins, Leonards
              Bērziņš, Pēteris Galiņš and Bruno Skulte. Symphonic com-
              positions were also in the program, notably Folk-dance
              Variations and Fugue by Tālivaldis Ķeniņš, which received
              the premiere of its orchestral version.

              A new approach in Latvian secondary education was initiated
              at the Latvian Center Garezers near Three Rivers, Michi-
              gan. It was based on the premise that a full high-school
              year can be compressed into an intensive eight-week sum-
              mer course, if the program is limited to select subjects
              pertaining to Latvian heritage, such as Latvian language,
              geography and history. This approach proved successful.
              The school has had a capacity enrollment of about 130 stu-
              dents since its second year of operation, and is in the pro-
              cess of expanding its facilities. Similar high schools now
              operate on both the East and West coasts.

              November 13. The Baltic Freedom Rally was held in New
              York City with an estimated fourteen thousand participants.
              A massive congregation of Estonians, Latvians and Lithu-
              anians from all parts of the U.S.A. gathered at Madison
              Square Garden for ceremonies followed by a march to the
              United Nations building. The aim of the demonstration was
              to call U.N. attention to Soviet imperialism in the Baltic
              states and the denial of human rights to Latvians, Lithuan-
              ians and Estonians in their native lands. Resolutions of the
              rally were delivered by Baltic delegates to Ambassadors of
              the U.N. This event marked the first large-scale joint Bal-
              tic effort in the U.S.A., and resulted in a permanent organ-
              ization, the Baltic Appeal to U.N. (BATUN).

              September. Over thirty new kokle players gathered in Phil-
              adelphia, Pennsylvania for the first kokle festival. Andrejs
              Jansons' Handbook for the Kokle Player was published on this

occasion. Less than five years before, there had been no
more than half a dozen players of the Latvian kokle in the
world, and perhaps all of three such instruments in this
country. The instrument was, however, rapidly gaining
popularity among young Latvian-Americans. By 1973 there
were about five hundred Latvian kokles in the U.S.A., with
at least three hundred of these owned by people actively
making music on them. Subsequently, kokle festivals have
become notable cultural events, hosted annually by Latvian
communities in the U.S.A. and Canada. They serve as a
forum for exchanging ideas and information on Latvian folk
music, as well as evaluating the artistic proficiency of individual participants and ensembles. Participants who play
their instruments at the festivals number from thirty-five
to sixty, depending on the general accessibility of the location.

The American Latvian Theater of Washington, D.C. toured
Latvian communities in the U.S.A. with Joks ir nopietna
lieta (Joke is a Serious Matter) by Mārtiņš Zīverts, giving
a total of eighteen performances.

The Latvian Evangelical Lutheran Church of Massachusetts
bought its own church.

Prof. Peter P. Lejins, director of the Institute of Criminal
Justice and Criminology at the University of Maryland, and
the long-term president of the American Latvian Association, was appointed by President Lyndon B. Johnson to a
six-year term as the U.S. correspondent to the United Nations in the realm of social defense. This is only one of
Prof. Lejins many appointments in criminology.

Jānis Annuss, Jr. received the H.W. Ranger Fund Purchase
Prize at the National Academy of Design Annuals in New
York.

1966   October 25. Resolution No. 416 calling on the president to
act on behalf of the Baltic states, having been approved by
the House 398 to 8, received Senate approval. This resolution was brought about by considerable pressure from the
Organization of the Americans for Congressional Action to
free the Baltic States.

Dr. Valdis Muižnieks negotiated with the University of Western Michigan in East Lansing, Michigan and arranged a lim-

ited Latvian non-credit program to be offered during the
summer session within the Department of Linguistics.
Since then courses in Latvian language and literature have
received full accreditation with the university and have had
an enrollment of more than two hundred students of both
Latvian and American descent. Dr. Jāzeps Lelis (Ph. D.
Harvard) from Howard University of Washington, D.C. and
Mrs. Lalita Muižnieks, with teaching assistants trained
within the program, provide a series of five courses in all
aspects of the Latvian language, from a beginner's course
to modern Latvian literature.

The Baltic Appeal to the United Nations (BATUN), later incorporated as the United Baltic Appeal, Inc. (UBA), was established in the wake of the Madison Square Garden Freedom Rally on November 13, 1965. UBA is an organization
representing the joint efforts of Latvians, Lithuanians and
Estonians to rekindle international concern for the Baltic
problems. Its functions are those of an independent information agency, without political or partisan alignment. Ultimately devoted to the restoration of self-determination
for Estonia, Latvia and Lithuania, its short-range goals
aim at arousing world public opinion on their behalf.
BATUN is a department of UBA, which focuses on the UN
as the appropriate international forum for discussion of the
Baltic issues. It maintains constant contact with diplomats
at the UN. Delegations of American Balts make formal visits to individual UN missions as well as to the UN Commission on Human Rights. BATUN observes closely the activities of the UN, and lobbies on behalf of Balts whenever per-
tinent issues come up on the agenda. BATUN also supplies
UN missions with information in memoranda and special
reports, emphasizing present conditions in the Baltic states
which violate specific provisions of the UN. Recently issued BATUN materials concern such topics as self-determination, ethnic discrimination, religious persecution, the
rights of minorities and the right to travel abroad and return to one's country. The UBA Information Service supplies
news releases for eight-five newspapers, radio programs,
international journalists and publications in an attempt to
overcome Western mass media silence about Baltic matters.
It also keeps the Baltic community and national publications
up to date concerning trends, functions and events at the
UN. UBA-BATUN operates an office in New York within
close proximity to the headquarters of the UN. Latvian
participation in this organization has been decisive. Rev.

N. Trepša (died in 1973) and Dr. Dzintars Paegle were
among its founders. Dagmāra Vallens, editor of UBA
publications and manager of its offices, is Latvian.

August 21. Following the resignation of Latvian Archbishop
Kārlis Kundziņš, Arnolds Lūsis, pastor of St. John's Latvian Evangelical Lutheran Church in Toronto, Canada, was
ordained in the highest office of the Latvian Evangelical
Lutheran Church in Exile in Seattle, Washington.

St. Paul's Latvian Evangelical Lutheran Church of Detroit,
Michigan, purchased it own church.

September. The Latvian Folk Ensemble of New York, directed by Andrejs Jansons, toured the U.S.A. and Canada
giving a total of thirteen performances.

Arvid Grant Associates of Olympia, Washington, received
the American Institute of Steel Construction Award for the
design of a bridge across the River Cle Elum in Kittitas
County. The company's Cascade Gardens Bridge over the
Wenachee River at Leavenworth received the Pressed Concrete Institute Special Award. A. Upesleja-Grants has
served as president of the Association of Structural Engineers of Washington State South-West Chapter.

Pauls Sakss (born in 1878 in Latvia), leading tenor of the
National Opera in Riga, Latvia, died in New York. He made
a concert tour of the U.S.A. in 1921, was on the faculties
of both the Conservatory of Latvia and the University of
Latvia, and conducted his own voice studio in New York in
the 1950's.

Uldis Baumanis, a violinist, received an M.M. degree from
the Manhattan School of Music. Baumanis is a concert soloist and teaches violin at the New York State Teachers' College.

1967   Many American Latvians, both privately and on an organized basis, vehemently protested the action by Great Britain
that disposed of Latvian gold reserves held in Great Britain
since 1940. Of the 13.45 million pounds of sterling belonging to the Republic of Latvia, a considerable amount was
transferred to the Soviet Union.

The Latvian Evangelical Lutheran Church Association in

America (LELDAA) held its first annual Latvian Youth for
Christ meeting at Latvian Center Garezers in Three Rivers,
Michigan.

The Philadelphia Society of Free Letts completed renova-
tions and the expansion designed by Mirdza Sēja Mediks for
the building, on the historical site that the organization had
owned since 1910.

The Latvian Boy Scout and Girl Scout camp Tēvzeme (Fatherland) was held in Garezers near Three Rivers, Michigan.

The American Latvian Theatre, Boston Ensemble, performed
Vara (Power) by Mārtiņš Zīverts six times.

The American Latvian Theater of Washington, D.C. toured
Latvian communities in the U.S.A. performing Jolanta Durbe
by Anšlavs Eglītis nineteen times.

Mazais Teātris (The Little Theatre) of San Francisco was
founded by Laimonis Siliņš. It has staged sixteen plays in
Latvian - twelve by Latvian authors and four translations.
Up to 1973, the troupe had given ninety-two performances,
nine of which were held in Toronto and Vancouver, Canada;
Laimonis and Biruta Siliņš gave dramatic performances on
a tour of Australia, and one performance in New Zealand.
The repertoire of the theater is drawn from a wide range
of dramatic literature. Its actors belong to the "younger
generation," trained outside Latvia. The theatre has also
staged Through the Brandenburg Gates by Anšlavs Eglītis
in English translation, and performed it for American audiences at the Comedia Theater in Palo Alto, California.

June 12. Voldemars Dobrovolskis (born in 1895 in Latvia),
a pianist, died in Chicago. He had taught at his piano studio
in Riga, and in the U.S.A. he taught at Roosevelt University in Chicago. He was a composer of songs, as well as
miniatures for the piano.

August 11. Ādolfs Ābele (born in 1889 in Latvia), a composer,
organist, conductor, and educator, died in Kalamazoo,
Michigan. In 1915 he had graduated from the Conservatory
of St. Petersburg, Russia, in organ and composition; from
1918 to 1924, he directed the Conservatory of Liepāja, Latvia; from 1924 to 1944 he was dean of the Latvian Conservatory of Music in Rīga. As the conductor of Dziesmuvara

(Song Power) from 1927 to 1944, a choir of the music honor
society of the University of Latvia, Ābele toured Baltic and
Scandinavian countries. In the U.S.A. since the 1950's,
Ābele was the honorary conductor of the Grand Choir at the
1958 New York Song Festival.

Artūrs Ozoliņš, concert pianist, completed piano studies
at the Mannes College of Music in New York. Ozoliņš had
graduated in 1962 from the Royal Conservatory of Toronto,
Canada and studied on scholarship at the University of Toronto and with Natalia Boulanger. In 1969 he won the first
prize in the young musicians' contest in Edmonton, Canada
and received first prize in the ninth annual Canadian radio
music festival. He is the recipient of a special award
from CBS to continue his music studies. Ozoliņš has appeared with several major orchestras, performing world
renowned compositions as well as the works of Latvian composers.

Juris Zvērs won the Bell System Correspondence Chess
Tournament over 800 participants.

1968   About twelve American Latvians in the U.S. armed forces
were killed during the Vietnam conflict. One of them,
Army Capt. Juris Šteinbergs, was awarded the Distinguished
Service Cross posthumously, and is buried in Arlington National Cemetery. Air Force First Lt. Artis Lielmanis was
awarded the Air Force Cross, also posthumously.

November 28-December 1. The first Baltic Studies Conference was held at the University of Maryland, featuring lectures, panel discussions and free discussion periods.
About 150 well-known scholars of Baltic descent participated
in the activities. At the end of this conference, the Association for the Advancement of Baltic Studies (AABS) was
founded in order to provide Baltic scholars with an appropriate forum for the pursuit and presentation of their research. It is an international,, non-profit organization,
which devotes its activities exclusively to scholarship. Its
publication, the Journal of Baltic Studies, edited by Dr. Arvīds Ziedonis, Jr., presents articles by social scientists
about Baltic questions pertaining to the Soviet-occupied
peoples as well as to Balts in the free world. The first
president of the AABS was Dr. Gundars J. King.

The seventeenth annual Congress of the American Latvian
Association was held in Washington, D.C., with ninety-

three participating delegates. At the same time the Washington Latvian community, together with the delegation of the ALA Congress, commemorated the fiftieth anniversary of Latvian independence on November 18, 1918. Religious services were officiated by Archbishop Arnolds Lūsis at the Washington National Cathedral. The ALA issued a commemorative brochure in three languages (English, French and Spanish), dealing with the history of Latvia over the past fifty years. A traveling exhibit, displaying Latvian cultural achievements, designed by Harijs Gricēvičs, was on view in many U.S. cities during this year.

The Latvian folk religion Dievturi held a service in conjunction with the song festival. (See page 70.) This was the largest Dievturi-sponsored event to take place in the U.S.A. It was presided by Arvīds Brastiņš, who had been among the founders of this religious movement, when it was organized in Latvia in 1925 and led by his brother Ernests Brastiņš. The dominant Dievturi orientation is ethical and aesthetic. Their ritual and beliefs are drawn from the Latvian dainas, ancient "godsongs" in folklore, which predate the introduction of Christianity among Latvians. Dievturi are active in the Chicago, Milwaukee, New York, Boston, and Philadelphia areas, as well as in Toronto, Canada. Their semiannual publication Labietis has appeared regularly since 1950. Literary, artistic and scholarly efforts from this group have done much to research, interpret and popularize many aspects of Latvian folklore.

The American Latvian Association instituted competitive examinations in elementary Latvian education. There are about fifty Latvian weekend schools in the U.S.A., with an approximate total of 2,500 students. These schools operate under the auspices of Latvian churches and local Latvian societies, but are coordinated by the Bureau of Education of the American Latvian Association. The curriculum of the supplementary schools at the elementary level is designed for children from four to thirteen years of age ranging from Kindergarten to the eighth grade. It calls for a total of 198 thirty-five minute lessons per school year for each class. The division of subject matter for each grade varies according to the child's age and level of comprehension. The subjects include religion, Latvian language, Latvian history, Latvian geography, folk songs and folk dance. This standard curriculum is followed within the realm of possibilities of the local Latvian communities, e.g. in some Latvian centers the school hours may be shorter, but the load of homework heavier. The selection of teachers

is based upon the formal educational qualfications gained
either in Latvia or abroad. The financial rewards for these
teachers are minimal; many teachers work on a voluntary
basis.

The fourth Latvian Song Festival was held in Cleveland,
Ohio. The grand choir numbered a record 1,100 singers,
and was directed by Bruno Skulte, Jānis Kalniņš, Arnolds
Kalnājs, Jānis Norvilis, Roberts Zuika. Jānis Kalniņš also
directed members of the Cleveland Orchestra in his own
New Brunswick Rhapsody, and Dziesmu vairogā (In the
Shield of Song) by Bruno Skulte. Antonina Vaivode rendered
the solo sections. A duet of the young soloists Dace Kārk-
liņa, soprano, and Jānis Barušs, tenor, in Jāņu vakars
(Midsummer Night) by Emils Melngailis highlighted the
grand concert. A special concert of new music premiered
instrumental compositions by Arnolds Šturms, Eduards Šēnfelds, Longins Apkalns and Vilnis Ciemiņš, and vocal works
by Voldemars Dobrovoļskis, Viktors Baštiks, Jānis Norvilis,
Longins Apkalns, and Eduards Šēnfelds. A concert of sacred music was held at the Cleveland Cathedral of the Holy
Trinity. The folk dance spectacular was directed by Elvīra
and Voldemārs Dzelme of Chicago and brought 700 young
dancers together. As a prelude to the folk program, the
dance artist Vija Vētra performed an interpretive solo containing elements of modern and Far-Eastern dances with
Latvian midsummer mythical symbolism. Miss Vētra, who
has studied dance in Europe and India, has a studio in New
York and travels widely in the U.S.A. demonstrating her
unique art for American audiences on college campuses and
elsewhere. The Folk Ensemble of New York was also a participant in the folk dance event. Atvadības (The Bride's
Departure), a stage musical arranged and directed by Lilija
Gleške, consisted exclusively of folk music and poetry dra-
matizing ancient Latvian wedding customs. The Washington,
D.C. and New York theater group staged Ugunī (In the Fire)
by Rūdolfs Blaumanis, directed by Osvalds Uršteins, starring Anda Uršteins.

The Latvian Folk Dance Association was established in
Cleveland, Ohio. Johanna Rinka, ethnologist and researcher
of folk dances in Latvia, and presently residing in the U.S.A.,
is an honorary member. This association standardizes the
authentic dance patterns, records new choreographed vari-
ants, maintains a library of both, and makes its materials
available to Latvian folk-dance groups throughout the U.S.A.
Outstanding leaders of folk-dance groups are Lidija Āboliņa

in Boston, Maija Mednis in Philadelphia, Alfrēds and Zi-
grīda Gaujenieks in New York, Irēna Beleičiks in Seattle,
Mirdza Paudrupe and Gundega Peniķis in Kalamazoo, Aija
Turaida in San Francisco, Mirdza Lapeniece in Los Angeles,
and Elvīra and Voldemārs Dzelme in Chicago.

The Latvian American Republican National Committee was
founded in Cleveland, Ohio. It was the first such political
organization of ethnic minorities established in the U.S.A.,
and was accepted by the Republican party. Voldemārs
Korsts of Chicago, Illinois, was elected its president. This
committee still operates and has expressed its standpoint
on numerous national and international policies introduced
by the U.S. government.

UBA-BATUN organized demonstrations at the United Nations
and elsewhere in New York City during the invasion of
Czechoslovakia by the armed forces of the Soviet Union.
UBA also initiated a massive letter writing and petition-
signing campaign during which individual Americans of Baltic descent wrote to different heads of states around the
world on the fiftieth anniversary of the declaration of independence of Estonia, Latvia and Lithuania.

The Latvian Evangelical Lutheran Church of Indianapolis,
Indiana, purchased its own church.

A conference on Baltic linguistics was held at Pennsylvania
State University. It was devoted exclusively to modern Latvian, Lithuanian, and the now extinct Old Prussian and was
probably the first such conference outside the Baltic republics.

July. The first issue of Latvju Mūzika (Latvian Music) appeared. This is an annual publication, edited by Valentīns
Bērzkalns, containing retrospective as well as current material on Latvian music. This journal is of high scholastic
quality and provides information about composers as well
as musicians. Of numerous musicians of Latvian descent
in the U.S.A., the best known are Žanis Dumpis - viola,
Rūdolfs Miķelsons - violin, Imants Gleške - violin, and
Jānis Ādamsons - cello, in Indianapolis; Andrejs Lindbergs
- violin and presently, librarian, and Franz Vlashek - cello
with the National Symphony Orchestra in Washington, D.C.;
Valdemārs Ruševics - violin, in Kalamazoo, Michigan; Eduards Vīnerts - violin, in Oakland, California; Andrejs Jansons - oboe, Dzidris Treimanis - cello, Arnolds Šturms -

flute, and Gundars Pone - composer, in New York; Norma
Auziņa - assistant concertmaster and violinist at the Eastman School of Music in Rochester, New York; Vilnis Baumanis - violin, in New Orleans, Louisiana. In addition,
Aldis Lagzdiņš, an accomplished organist, and Anda Zirnīte,
a young and gifted pianist are among the already widely acclaimed musicians representing the younger generation,
who have received their musical education in the U.S.A.
July-August. The Latvian Folk Ensemble of New York, directed by Andrejs Jansons, toured Western Europe: giving
one performance and participating in a BBC radio broadcast
in London; giving three concerts in Hanover, West Germany;
and performing in radio broadcasts in Berne, Switzerland.
This tour continued in the U.S.A. with more performances
in Cleveland and Poughkeepsie, New York.

The American Latvian Theatre of Washington, D.C., toured
the U.S.A. with Ugunī (In the Fire) by Rūdolfs Blaumanis,
giving a total of nine performances.

Prof. Peter Lejins of the University of Maryland was named
editor-in-chief of the Journal of Research in Crime and De-
linquency.

A. Liepnieks was elected the regional vice-president of the
U.S. Chess Federation.

The University of Missouri in Rolla, Missouri, named its
electrochemical laboratory after Mārtiņš Straumanis (1898-
1973), the noted research professor of metallurgical engineering. His more than three hundred articles have been
published in scientific journals in English and other languages. Together with Prof. Bruno Jirgensons, he published
a textbook in nuclear chemistry, which has been translated
into German, Spanish, and Japanese. In 1967 Straumanis received a research award at the University of Missouri, and
the National Association of Corrosion Engineers gave him
the Rodney Willis Whitney Award for his achievements in
corrosion engineering.

Latvian artist Jānis Cīrulis gained recognition as a medical
illustrator. Mankind in Making was published with Cīrulis'
illustrations. He is employed at the Childrens Hospital in
Boston.

Atis (Pete) Pētersons, assistant manager of Southern Cali-

fornia Striders Track & Field Club was elected coach for
the U.S. olympic track and field team at Lake Tahoe. Bill
Toomey, trained by Pētersons, won the gold medal in shot-
put at the Mexico City Olympic Games. The following year
Pētersons served as assistant coach for the U.S. track and
field team that competed against the Soviet Union and British teams. Pētersons also coached and acted as assistant
manager for the U.S. track and field team competing in the
Soviet Union, Europe and Africa in 1973.

Alfrēds Bērziņš (born in 1899), author of The Two Faces of
Co-Existence (1967) and The Unpunished Crime (1962) in
English, dealing with the communist take-over of Latvia,
received the International Latvian Award. Bērziņš was the
minister of the interior of Latvia's last government, and
the only member of Ulmanis' cabinet to reach the free world.
Bērziņš remained a leading political figure of Latvians in
exile. In the U.S.A., he has served on the Committee for
a Free Latvia, and as a member of the board of the World
Federation of Free Latvians and the American Latvian Association.

October 27. Peter Meezitt, proprietor of Weston Nurseries
in Hopkinton, Massachusetts, died. Meezitt had received
numerous prizes at the Annual Boston Spring Flower Shows
throughout his long horticultural career. He was nationally
known as the developer of new rhododendron varieties. His
business is now administered by his son, Edmond Meezitt.

1969 July 4. Māra Kristberga-Culp (born in 1941 in Rīga) won
first place at the twenty-third annual U.S. Powder-Puff
Derby, flying her lightweight Piper aircraft from San Diego,
California, to Washington, D.C. in a record time of 11 hours
and 57 minutes, and was honored at a White House reception for women pilots by Mrs. Richard M. Nixon.

The concert season of 1969-1970 in the U.S. Latvian communities offered about one hundred major concerts in such
Latvian centers as New York, Milwaukee, Chicago, Cleveland, Kalamazoo, San Francisco, Grand Rapids, and Philadelphia. About half of these concerts were solo recitals;
the remainder featured choirs or other types of musical ensembles.

By this year, about one hundred young musicians had received music degrees from higher educational institutions

in the free world, including the U.S.A. They comprise
about 0.06% of all Latvians outside Latvia today.

September. The Latvian Folk Ensemble of New York toured
U.S. eastern and central states giving a total of eight performances.

The American Latvian Theatre, Boston Ensemble, performed a Latvian translation of The Sacred Flame by W.
Somerset Maugham in Boston and New York City. This production also toured Willimantic, Connecticut and Toronto,
Ontario.

Dr. Edward Anders participated in the moon-rock analysis
at the University of Chicago, Illinois.

October. The Latvian Folk Ensemble of New York participated in a musical, Koklētājs un velns (the Kokle-Player
and the Devil) by Bruno Skulte of New York, which premiered in Toronto, Canada. This musical was based on
Latvian folk tales about a kokle player and his encounter
with the underworld. It was well received by the Latvian
audiences in Canada, as well as during its subsequent performances in the U.S.A. Skulte's score represents one of
the original compositions especially created for the kokle
and accompanying instruments. Because of the renaissance
of this ancient instrument, many other modern Latvian composers have been inspired to write original music for kokle.

Staņislavs Reinis was elected as one of four councilmen of
Cedar Rapids, Iowa. An agronomist educated in Latvia and
Germany, Reinis is in charge of Cedar Rapids' parks, wood-
land, play and recreational area planning and maintenance.
He has been responsible for ten thousand newly planted trees
in this city. He has established new parks and generally
given Cedar Rapids the appearance of a garden city. Cedar
Rapids Airport boasts extensive flowerbed arrangements,
which earned it the first place prize for beautification among
U.S. airports.

December 2. Bishop Jāzeps Rancāns (born in Nautrāni, Latvia in 1886) died in Grand Rapids, Michigan. In 1919 Rancāns had been a delegate to the Holy See and arranged a con-
cordat between Latvia and the Holy See. Elevated to bishop
in 1924, Rancāns served as a professor of theology at the
University of Latvia until 1940. He had also held political

office and had been vice-chairman of the last three elected
Latvian parliaments.

Andrejs Jagars, Sr., (born in 1892 in Latvia) an electrical
engineer, died in Washington, D.C. Educated at the Elec-
trotechnical Institute in St. Petersburg, Russia, Jagars was
the chief engineer of Latvia's telephone and telegraph service during the nation's independence. After his arrival in
the U.S.A. in 1951, Jagars worked as an electrical maintenance man, but soon joined the Washington firm of Pamero,
and became chief electrical designer for projects at the
Armed Forces Institute of Pathology, the U.S. Capitol and
the Library of Congress. Since 1961 he has been with the
office of the Architect of the Capitol, responsible for de-
signing, constructing and maintaining all congressional
buildings. Two Latvians were involved in the 1960 award-
winning conversion project of the U.S. Capitol and the expansion of the building's east wing. Jagars was the chief
electrical designer, while architect Verners Švalbe, a Latvian of a younger generation, educated at Columbia University, was on the professional team in charge of the project's
architectural aspects. Laima Kalniņš, the daughter of Andrejs Jagars, Sr. and herself an architect, has planned the
Park Police headquarters in Washington, D.C., the maintenance unit on MacArthur Boulevard near the Georgetown
water reservoir, and several other recreational buildings
for the D.C. Recreational Department. One of her draw-
ings can be viewed at the Ford Theater Museum, where she
has worked in its historical research. Jagars' son, Andrejs
Jagars, Jr. is an engineer involved with the planning of the
Washington, D.C. Metro system, under construction since
1970.

Dr. Valda Melngaile-Dreimane was the first woman to hold
a post on the Board of Executives of the American Latvian
Association. Dr. Melngaile served as the chairman of the
Bureau of Culture. She received her Ph.D. in German from
Harvard University, Cambridge, Massachusetts. She
teaches German at Boston University and has lectured at numerous Latvian educational events, such as 2 x 2 and the
summer high schools at Garezers in Michigan and Beverīna
in Pennsylvania. Dr. Melngaile published one volume of
poetry in Latvian, Ūdens raksti (Water Ripples), in 1970.

February 9. The first flight of the Boeing 747, the world's
largest passenger plane at that time. The Latvian engineer

Edvīns Circenis had been in charge of developing the plans
for the wing construction. Several Latvian engineers were
involved in this and other projects of the Boeing Company
in Seattle, Washington, including Viktors Otlāns' firm that
subcontracted with Boeing, and Viesturs Zommers, who is
a Boeing sales representative in Europe.

Architect Kārlis Grīnbergs patented his "Karlis structures,"
a type of "do-it-yourself," multi-purpose interior shelving
system, utilizing three basic components with wide ranging
design possibilities in their combination. "Karlis Structures" and Grīnbergs' unusual Jamaica Plain, Massachusetts
home - a remodeled farm building - had been featured in a
1968 issue of American Home. Latvian-born Grīnbergs was
fifteen when he arrived in the U.S.A. in 1950. He is a part-
ner of Buckminster Fuller Architects and in charge of the
company's design for the major airport of India, in New
Delhi.

Olafs Zeidenbergs (born in 1937 in Aizpute, Latvia), a graduate of the Yale School of Architecture and a professor of
art at Southern Connecticut College, won the New Britain,
Connecticut competition for a fountain design to be erected
in its Leo A. Milewski Park. Zeidenbergs is the winner of
numerous other art awards for sculptures exhibited in the
state of Connecticut. In 1970 Zeidenbergs won the top award
at the annual New England Exhibit of Painting and Sculpture.

Guntis Baltābols played in the U.S. Army Volleyball All-
Stars.

1970   According to 1970 census data, there were 86,413 Latvian-
Americans residing in the United States. Of these, 41,707
were foreign-born Latvians, and 44,706 were American
nationals of foreign or mixed parentage. The ten states
with the largest number of American Latvians were New
York - 16,433; California - 9,769; Illinois - 8,318; New Jersey - 5,164; Massachusetts - 5,100; Pennsylvania - 4,946;
Michigan - 4,935; Ohio - 4,589; Wisconsin - 2,649; and
Maryland - 2,640, closely followed by Connecticut, Florida,
and Minnesota.

The American Latvian Association held its nineteenth annual
congress in Indianapolis, Indiana with 101 participating delegates. This congress elected a new president, Uldis Grava
of New York, representing the emergence of a younger gen-

eration in the leadership of Latvians in America. He succeeded Prof. Peter Lejins, who had been an outstanding
leader for many years; Prof. Lejins is still an active honorary president of the association.

The third Regional Latvian Song Festival of the West Coast
was held in Los Angeles, California with over two hundred
singers participating. The grand concert was conducted by
Olǧerts Bištēviņš, Arvīds Berķis, Ernests Brusubārda, Jr.,
and Pēteris Galiņš. In addition, there was a separate concert with many soloists participating, performing works of
several Latvian composers. The Los Angeles theatre performed Minhauzena precĪbas by Anšlavs Eglītis, under the
direction of Vilis Lapenieks. On the lighter side, the Čikagas PiecĪši gave a performance of contemporary vocal
music, consisting mainly of satirical music.   In addition
to musical events, the traditional arts and crafts exhibit
was held, contemporary writers and poets presented their
works in a literary program, and folk dance groups performed at a special show.

The Latvian Freedom Fountain, designed by a Latvian artist, Ansis Bērziņš, was dedicated in Colorado Springs, Colorado. It bears the following inscription: "The Latvian
Freedom Fountain is a gift from the Latvian ethnic group to
the people of Colorado Springs, commemorating in 1968 the
50th anniversary of the Declaration of Independence of Latvia. Since 1949, thousands of Latvian refugees have found
freedom and opportunity in the United States. This fountain
is a symbol of hope for all of the formerly free people of
the world who keep alive in their hearts the hope of self-
determination under God for all nations."

Voldemārs Korsts of Chicago, Illinois was one of seventeen
Republican nationality leaders appointed to the U.S. Department of State Special Advisory Commission on Public Opinion. He was further appointed chairman of the Policies and
Resolutions Committee of the National Republican Heritage
(Nationalities) Council. This committee frequently ex-
presses the importance of the Baltic states' freedom to over-
all peace and stability of the world.

The Latvian Foundation was established at the initiative of
Dr. Valdis Muižnieks of Kalamazoo, Michigan. This is an
attempt to finance the cultural and educational needs of a
society such as the Latvian community in the U.S.A., which

has no authority to tax its membership and secure a permanent source of income. The foundation is based upon loans from private individuals, families and organizations who are willing to forfeit interest on the sum of their contributions. The foundation applies this borrowed capital to investments which yield a return to the user exclusively for financing various Latvian cultural projects. By early 1973 the foundation had a membership of 350 and a capital of eighty-two thousand dollars; actively promoted, the foundation is expected to grow at a similar pace toward its capitalization goal of one million dollars. In its second year of operation the foundation financed two projects with a composite sum of $2,500.00: a book for the teaching of Latvian using structural linguistics by Dr. Jāzeps Lelis and Dzidra Liepiņa, and a dictionary of Latvian phonology by Dr. Velta Rūķe-Draviņa. The foundation's membership votes for the projects to be financed each year.

October 18. Baltic demonstrations took place at the United Nations in New York City, commemorating the twenty-fifth anniversary of the United Nations and demanding human rights and self-determination for the Baltic nations in the Soviet Union. The Baltic Youth for Freedom, comprised of young Americans of Latvian, Estonian and Lithuanian descent, continued the demonstration for a week, riding a Baltic truck through the streets of New York City under the slogan "Free the Baltic Three!" The Baltic Youth for Freedom is noted for its small-scale efforts that attract public notice through pointed slogans and colorful street demonstrations. They respond quickly to current events and have demonstrated in New York City on such occasions as the invasion of Czechoslovakia, Simas Kudirka's extradition, Lithuanian riots in Kaunas, Lithuania, the Soviet art exhibit at the Metropolitan Museum, and the visit of Leonid Brezhnev to Washington, D.C.

October 25. The Baltic Youth for Freedom protested in New York because of consistent failure of the New York press to report Baltic events.

November 23. A Lithuanian seaman, Simas Kudirka, attempted to defect from the Soviet Union by jumping from his Soviet ship onto the U.S. Coast Guard cutter Vigilant, while both were located within U.S. territorial waters. Kudirka was refused asylum and Russians were allowed to board the Vigilant in order to return the defector by force.

An American-Latvian, Robert M. Brieže, president of the
New Bedford Seafood Producers' Association, was present
on the Russian ship, where fishing negotiations were taking
place, in which he represented the U.S. seafood industry.
Brieže witnessed the incident, tried to intervene on behalf
of Kudirka, and was probably instrumental in bringing this
incident to the attention of the American press. Kudirka
was tried in the Soviet Union in May 1971 and sentenced to
ten years of hard labor.

November - December. Americans of Baltic descent in New
York and elsewhere protested the extradition of Simas Kudirka to Soviet authorities.

Daina Pālēna from Soviet Latvia requested political asylum
with U.S. authorities, and the Immigration Department
granted her the right to remain in the U.S.A. Pālēna, an
employee aboard a Soviet vessel docked in New York harbor,
was brought into the city to receive medical first aid after
having taken an overdose of aspirin.

UBA-BATUN organized a Baltic Folk Festival on the Latvian-
owned site Priedaine (Place of Pines) in New Jersey. This
was the first of such annual fund-raising events, which provide opportunities for Americans of Baltic descent to
strengthen their social and cultural ties.

The Latvian Folk Dance Association held a Latvian folk-
dance seminar at the Latvian Center Garezers (Long Lake)
near Three Rivers, Michigan. Another such seminar was
held in 1971.

Laimons Eglītis won the top award at the Atlantic City national art exhibit. His drawing Two Sources was purchased
by the Philadelphia Museum of Art for its permanent collection.

The Latvian artist Harijs Gricēvičs designed a striking out-
door pavillion on the lawn of the White House, in which a
garden party was held in honor of Prince Charles and Prin-
cess Anne of Great Britain during their summer visit to the
U.S.A.

Mārtiņš Šlessers published a well-noted article "Bathing
Methods of Song Birds" in the American Ornithological
Union Magazine, featuring some excellent colored illustra-
tions.

Aldis Lagzdiņš of New York won the first prize in the Youth
Organist Competition in the U.S.A. He had also received
the first prize at the competition of the National Guild of
American Organists in Denver, Colorado in 1968, and was
the first organist to receive the Erskine Prize at the Julliard
School of Music.

1971   The annual congress of the American Latvian Association
was held in Grand Rapids, Michigan, with ninety-nine participating delegates. It also commemorated the twentieth
anniversary of the American Latvian Association in the
U.S.A. A White House aide addressed the congress on behalf of the president of the United States.

The UBA-BATUN delivered petitions with thirteen thousand
signatures to the United Nations High Commission for Refugees, demanding the release of Simas Kudirka.

St. Paul's Latvian Evangelical Lutheran Church of Maywood,
Illinois built its own church.

The American Latvian Theatre of Washington, D.C. toured
the U.S.A. and Canada performing Bezkaunīgie veči (The
Daring Old Men) by Anšlavs Eglītis twenty-one times.

The American Latvian Theatre, Boston Ensemble, gave
four performances of Nebrauc tik dikti (Take it easy! or,
Don't drive so fast!) by Jānis Lejiņš in Boston, New York,
Willimantic and Toronto.

May. The Latvian Kokle Ensemble, directed by Andrejs
Jansons, toured Western Europe and gave nine performances
in the following cities: Nottingham, London and Bradford
in England; Hamburg, Munster, Monchengladbach, and Stutt-
gart in Western Germany; and Goteburg and Stockholm in
Sweden. Its performances on this tour were favorably reviewed in the Latvian press as well as in the newspapers of
the respective cities abroad.

Daumants Hāzners of New Jersey was appointed a member
of the Highway Safety Commission by President Richard M.
Nixon.

Ģirts Puriņš of Pittsburgh, Pennsylvania, received a grant
from the University of Pittsburgh to study Latvian art in
Rīga, Latvia. During the 1960's he studied in Chicago and

sang with Čikagas Piecīši. Presently, he teaches painting, composition and color theory at Pittsburgh University. An exhibit of Puriņš' special compositions opened the 1973 season at the Carnegie Institute Art Museum. At the same time his work was also on view at the Westmoreland County Museum of Art and the Pittsburgh Plan for Art Gallery in Pennsylvania.

Gvido Augusts originated a half-hour color telecast "Augusts, 1971 Landscapes" seen over several ABC and NBC networks in the northwestern United States.

A. Kārkliņš became the chess champion of Illinois. Together with Jānis Tums, he won first place in the North Central chess tournament and placed second in the California Lone Tree chess tournament.

Gundar J. King, professor and dean of the School of Business Administration at Pacific Lutheran University, became president of the Western Association of Collegiate Schools of Business, a regional affiliate of the A.C.S.B., representing over sixty business school deans.

Marine officer Juris Luziņš won the eight-hundred meter run in the American Athletic Union track and field championships.

Ernests Venta and Guntis Baltābols were members of the U.S. National Volleyball Team.

Rein Kampersal (born in 1888 in Latvia) a Latvian philanthropist and the owner of Kampersal's Dairy in Rolliston, Maryland, died.

1972   The Executive Board of Directors of the World Federation of Free Latvians met for the first time en toto in Elka Park, New York. They represented Europe, Australia, Canada, South America, and the United States. They adapted a new slogan for the World Federation of Free Latvians - "Latvia for Latvians and Latvians for Latvia!" They also affirmed an ancient Latvian fertility symbol, Jumis, as the representative sign of all Latvians that express the demand of modern Latvians to prosper in their own land. This symbol has become popular throughout the free world among all age groups of Latvians.

The Latvian Relief Fund of America celebrated its twentieth year of operation. The fund's financial progress over the two decades reflects the growing prosperity of the Latvian immigrant community in the U.S.A. In its founding year, the fund had a budget of two thousand dollars; the budget of 1972 surpassed the one-million-dollar mark. The total benefits paid out by the fund during its twenty years is about six million dollars. The original life insurance benefits amounted to two hundred dollars per member. Today, an individual can subscribe to a maximum policy of twenty-five hundred dollars. Hospitalization benefits were likewise limited to two hundred dollars a year, and have subsequently been increased to a maximum of six thousand dollars.

The twentieth annual congress of the American Latvian Association was held in Cleveland, Ohio, with eighty-four participating delegates. Dr. Ilgvars J. Spilners from Pittsburgh, Pennsylvania was elected as the new president.

The UBA-BATUN delegation presented the U.S. mission to the United Nations with petition signatures gathered by the Baltic Youth for Freedom opposing President Richard M. Nixon's visit to Moscow.

Americans of Baltic descent demonstrated at the UN building and elsewhere in New York on the occasion of the Lithuanian riots in Soviet-occupied Kaunas, Lithuania.

The eleventh Latvian Press Congress was held at Elka Park, New York; it passed a resolution condemning harassments and persecution of writers in Soviet Latvia.

The Metropolitan Museum of New York received a donation made to its folk costume division and library by Mrs. Amanda Liberte-Rebāne, (wife of Ludolfs Liberts): two authentic regional Latvian costumes - those of Bārta and Nīca. M.J. Krastiņš supplied the costume library with a collection of slides depicting Latvian regional dress.

The Latvian Boy Scout and Girl Scout camp Rīga dimd was held in Toronto, Canada, where numerous representatives of all-Latvian boy and girl scout troops in the U.S.A. participated.

The Latvian Evangelical Lutheran Church of Elizabeth and Newark, New Jersey, purchased its own church.

The Latvian Evangelical Lutheran Church of Washington, D.C., purchased a two-acre property in Rockville, Maryland for the eventual site of a new church and a social hall.

The American Latvian Theatre of Washington, D.C., toured Latvian communities in the U.S.A. and Canada performing Tagad ir citādi (It's different now) by Artūrs Straumanis twenty times.

Prof. Peter Lejins, the former president of the American Latvian Association and a professor of sociology and criminology at the University of Maryland, was renamed by President Richard M. Nixon to the post of U.S. correspondent in the United Nations Program for the Prevention of Crime and Treatment of Offenders for a term of three years.

Dr. Edgar Andersons, a Latvian historian and professor at San Jose State University, author of twelve books and sixty articles in various American and European scholarly magazines and recipient of many American, European and West Indian research grants, was named the Outstanding Educator of America for 1972. He has done extensive research and lectured in many American, European, West Indian and Australian universities and institutions. From 1970 to 1973, he served first as vice-president and later as president of the Association for Advancement of Baltic Studies (AABS) and has held various scientific positions.

Dr. Sigurds Grava was commissioned by the City of New York to develop a master plan for its metropolitan transportation system. Grava heads the City Planning Department at Columbia University. His approach to transportation problems is concerned with the rights of pedestrians and cyclists, as well as patterns of motorized transportation. To practice what he preaches, he travels in New York by bicycle. Dr. Grava is also a United Nations advisor on city planning and has worked on the transportation systems of numerous metropolitan areas abroad, such as that of Karachi in Pakistan. He was also cofounder of AABS.(See page 68.)

A. Liepnieks, the promoter of chess among Latvians, assisted Fred Cramer, Bobby Fisher's manager, in Reykyavik, Iceland, during the famous world chess match between Boris Spasky and Bobby Fisher.

The Valley Forge Freedom Foundation, whose honorary

chairman presently is President Nixon, awarded the George
Washington medal of honor to Dr. Karl Leyasmeyer for his
presentation entitled "The Advancing World Menace and
How to Meet It." Since his arrival in the U.S.A., more
than twenty years ago, Dr. Leyasmeyer has been guest
speaker at over 450 colleges and universities, over 3,500
meetings and over 400 radio and television broadcasts. Dr.
Leyasmeyer's speeches are analyses of communism based
on his personal experiences during the Communist takeover
of Latvia in 1940; they also evaluate the role of religion in
the preservation of Western freedom.

Dr. Bruno Kalniņš, leader of the Social Democratic party
of the Republic of Latvia, and author of numerous books,
now living in exile in Sweden, made a speaking tour of U.S.
Latvian communities. His topics dealt with international
political relations and current circumstances in Latvia.
Imants Freimanis, likewise a leader of the Latvian community in Sweden, visited the U.S.A. and spoke at various
Latvian centers. Similarly, Ādolfs Šilde, the representative of Latvian Red Cross in West Germany, Dr. Dietrich
Loeber, professor of international law at the University of
Kiel, West Germany, Jānis Andrups, a literary scholar residing in Great Britain, Andrejs Eglītis, a noted Latvian
poet, and Mārtiņš Zīverts, a noted Latvian writer, both residing in Sweden, lectured throughout the U.S.A. to Latvian
audiences on cultural, political and literary topics.

Dr. Arvīds Ziedonis, director of Russian Studies at Mueh-
lenbach College, was a member of a four-man U.S. delegation to Moscow in preparation for the U.S.-Russian Citizens
and Educational Exchange Convention to be held in Moscow
in 1973. Dr. Ziedonis has been selected to head the Secre-
tariat of the projected convention and supervise the American delegation of some five hundred representatives of various professional, industrial, and academic fields.

Case Western Reserve University in Cleveland, Ohio, expanded its sociology department with a new study program
dealing with the problem of deprived, emotionally disturbed,
and physically neglected children in our society. Dr. Ilga
Švecha-Zemzare was in charge of this new study area at the
University. Dr. Švecha-Zemzare had taught at Case Western University for several years in the School of Medicine
and the Department of Sociology; in addition, she headed the
county government program of social therapy for neglected
children.

Andrejs Akermanis, a graduate of Mangaļi Marine Academy,
Latvia, and founder of A.O.A., Inc., of Florida, patented
an underwater scythe designed to mow the proliferating sea-
weed of Florida's swamp areas. There was a large and
immediate market for this tool, which is only one of Akermanis' numerous inventions for alleviating various water-
connected labors - including oars that contain first-aid
equipment, a collapsible ladder for deep-sea divers, and
an achoring device that adjusts to tidal variations.

The American National Council for Latvian Heritage Foundation was established for the advancement of Latvian cultural activities. Among its members are noted American
personalities, such as former Governor Furcolo of Massachusetts.

The town of Turtle Lake, North Dakota (15,000 inhabitants)
honored Dr. Haralds Kuplis, its only medical doctor, who
has worked at the town's hospital since 1952, and has expanded its facilities from fourteen to forty-four beds. Dr.
Kuplis is a graduate of the University of Latvia School of
Medicine.

Architect Ēriks Krūmiņš was appointed to the post of Milwaukee County Architect, whose office is responsible for
the construction and maintenance of old public buildings
throughout the county. Krūmiņš is a graduate of the University of Illinois and a leader in the Latvian community: its
church council, scout troop and other organizations.

The Architectural firm Gunnar Birkerts and Associates
started work on the ninth District Federal Reserve Bank in
downtown Minneapolis. Birkerts' design for the ten-story
steel structure, dubbed the "bridge-building," was hailed
by the press as one of the most unusual constructions being
built anywhere in the world. The first floor will begin
thirty feet above the ground and the whole structure will be
suspended between two huge pillars (two hundred feet high).
These will eliminate the need for interior collumns and provide unprecedented expansion of office space. Birkerts,
(born in 1925 in Latvia), is on the architectural faculty at
the University of Michigan, a member of the American Institute of Architects and a designer of several notable buildings in the Detroit area.

The Freedom Foundation at Valley Forge, Pennsylvania,

awarded its gold medal to Tedis Zieriņš, who had been a
recipient of this same award in 1970. He is an untiring
demonstrator against communist tyranny; his effective commercial posters and letters to editors have rarely failed to
arouse public notice.

July. Dr. Arnolds Spekke, Charge d'affaires of the Latvian
Legation in Washington, D.C., died after a long and serious illness.

During July, an original musical Meža teika (Forest Tale),
based on Latvian folklore, and composed by Andrejs Jansons, was performed at the Latvian summer camp at Elka
Park, New York. Stage decorations, exclusively of forest
materials, were designed by the acclaimed Latvian artist
Jānis Annuss.

August. The United Nations Institute of Training and Research, together with leading international organizations of
library scientists, held a conference in Geneva, Switzerland
This converence was devoted to problems of the global information and documentation expansion. Among the two hundred
participating experts from fifty countries was Ādolfs Sprūdžs,
a Latvian, in charge of the International Law Library of
Chicago University. Mr. Sprūdžs was invited to address
the conference on the legal status of multilateral treaties.

October. Māra Ozoliņš was selected to serve as a White
House social aide. Ms. Ozoliņš is a graduate of Berkeley,
the Air Force Academy in Texas, and Officer's Training
School in Mississippi. Prior to her White House appointment she worked at Air Force bases in California and
the Philippines.

October 28-29. The Second Conference on Baltic Literature
was held at Ohio State University in Columbus, Ohio.
Twenty scholarly papers were presented on subjects dealing
with historical and current aspects of Latvian, Lithuanian,
and Estonian Literature. Latvian scholars participating
with papers were Dr. Edgar Andersons, Dr. Vaira Vīķe-
Freibergs, Dr. Juris Silenieks, Gunārs Saliņš, Dr. Valters
Nollendorfs, Astrīda Ivask, and Dr. Valda Melngailis.

November 18. The Baltic World Conference was founded in
New York. The conference unites the highest representatives of the international organizations of Latvians, Eston-

ians and Lithuanians in the free world. Its purpose is to facilitate cooperation between the three nationalities, to undertake united political action, and to exchange information about circumstances in their occupied lands. The three member nationalities expect to coordinate administrative matters and establish a common agency for the dissemination of information.

November 30. Norberts J. Trepša (born in 1913 in Latvia), a Roman Catholic priest, author, lawyer, political theorist, and social organizer, died in New York. Under the pseudonym N. Neikšānīts, he wrote novels, poetry, and short prose in the Latgalian dialect of the Latvian language, and contributed to three papers: Lotgolas Vords, Zīdūnis, and Brīvā Zeme. He held academic degrees in philosophy, theology and sociology. In 1953 in Detroit, Michigan, he was ordained a priest of the Roman Catholic Church. He was also an editor of a Catholic publication, Dzimtenes balss, in Chicago between 1958 and 1962. Trepša was best known as the founder and first president of BATUN (Baltic Appeal to United Nations) and for related activities on behalf of Baltic international relations during the 1960's in New York.

1973   The fifth Latvian Song Festival commemorating the one hundredth anniversary of the first Song Festival held in Rīga, Latvia in 1873, was held in Cleveland, Ohio. In 1873 the first general Latvian Song Festival generated tremendous popular response, coming, as it did, during the national awakening of Latvians. In the summer of 1973, centennial song festivals were held in Rīga, Latvia, Cologne, West Germany; and Cleveland, Ohio. A conservative estimate of the attendance at the festival in Cleveland was fifteen thousand Latvians from all the free world. On behalf of President Richard M. Nixon, the opening ceremonies were attended by Julie Nixon Eisenhower, who addressed the Latvian audience on the advantages of possessing an ancient cultural heritage. Mrs. Eisenhower toured the fine arts exhibit as well as the ethnic crafts show, and received a token gift - a hand-crafted, amber-inlaid silver brooch. The mayor of Cleveland, Ralph J. Perk, had declared Latvian Song Days in the city and presented keys to the city of Cleveland to Andrejs Eglītis, a Latvian poet from Sweden, and Kaspars Svenne, conductor of the grand concert, from Australia. The series of concerts began with opening ceremonies at which a select choir rendered songs from the pro-

gram of the original festival one hundred years ago. The
grand concert, combining fifty-two choirs, was highlighted
by a cantata commissioned for this occasion: Sasauc, dzie-
sma! (Song Summons!), music by Helmârs Pavasars,
text by Andrejs Eglītis. This title bears also the motto of
the entire festival. Conductors of the grand concert were
Ernests Brusubārda, Jānis Kalniņš, Arnolds Kalnājs, Kaspars Svenne, and Roberts Zuika. Līna Karlsons (soprano)
and Irma Kurmiņš (soprano) were soloists. A concert of
religious music offered the premiere of a fugue-fantasia
Karavīri bēdājās (Soldier's Despair) by Arnolds Kalnājs.
Arvīds Purvs directed the choirs and orchestra; Anita Run-
dāne was organist; Rita Dzilna-Zaprauska and Astra Kalniņa
were the sopranos. Another work heard in America for the
first time was Kingiras rekviems (Requiem of Kingira) for
a choir, two soloists, organ and orchestra, by Longins Apkalns, blending a folk melody, bitonal harmonies, and do-
decaphonic structures. This work is a memorial to the
Latvian women who attempted a desperate uprising from
captivity in a Siberian forced-labor camp in 1954. A symphony concert was conducted by Jānis Kalniņš, whose third
symphony received its premiere at this occasion. Voldemārs Ruševics was concertmaster; the pianist performing
the solo part of Tālivaldis Ķeniņš' Fantasies Concertantes
was Artūrs Ozoliņš.

Folk dancing at this festival was featured at two events,
both directed by Lidija Āboliņa of Boston. For the first time,
a special presentation was devoted to choreographed, interpretive Latvian dances, loosely based on the style and spirit
of authentic Latvian folk dancing. Eighteen dance groups premiered twenty-five original numbers with choreographies
and musical arrangements created for this occasion. The
second event, the folk dance spectacular held at the Cleveland Arena gathered nine hundred dancers in a repertoire
of authentic folk dances drawn from ethnographic records of
folk traditions in Latvia. Extending the range of Latvian
song festivals to include folk dancing is a recent development. The first folk dance spectacular in America took
place at the Toronto Song Festival of 1961, with two hundred
dancers. Folk dance shows have since become an intrinsic
popular part of the festival, attracting audiences second
only to those of the grand choral concerts.

Two plays were presented by the Little Theater of San
Francisco, directed by Laimonis Siliņš. Galma gleznotājs
(The Court Artist in Residence) by Anšlavs Eglītis and Pazu-
dušais dēls (Prodigal Son) by Rūdolfs Blaumanis. A musical

play Jāņu nakts by Lilija Gleške was staged. Three writers'
seminars took place, featuring currently written prose and
poetry rendered in personal appearances by nearly forty
prominent Latvian authors. In addition to the public events,
religious services and more than thirty special interest
groups met during the festival, representing the entire spec-
trum of activities pursued in Latvian communities in the
U.S.A.

The American Latvian Theatre, Boston Ensemble, toured
the U.S.A. and Canada with Minchauzena precĪbas by Mārtiņš ZĪverts, giving a total of six performances.

The Latvian Folk Ensemble of New York directed by Andrejs Jansons gave four performances in the U.S.A. and
Canada.

The Latvian High School Ensemble from Münster, West
Germany, made an extensive tour through the U.S.A. and
Canada and performed a musical show based on folk mate-
rial for Latvian audiences.

Prof. Mārtiņš Straumanis, a world authority on metallurgy
and a member of the faculty of the University of Missouri,
died.

Pēteris EglĪtis (born in 1884, Latvia) died in New York. He
was an attorney at law of Latvia, and a long-time president
of the governing board of the Evangelical Lutheran Church
of Latvia and later, the Church in Exile.

A. Liepnieks, the Latvian chess promoter and editor of the
Latvian periodical Šacha pasaule (Chess World) died in
Lincoln, Nebraska.

Guna KalmĪte presented a one-person show of her paintings
in Chicago, Illinois, and received excellent reviews in the
local Chicago press. She also published a book of reproduc-
tions and evaluations of her father's, Jānis KalmĪte's, paintings. This is the first professional treatment in English of
a Latvian painter's work.

Capt. Fricis Strobels, U.S. Army, was decorated with the
first oak leaf cluster.

The Joint Latvian Organizations of Los Angeles built a Latvian community center.

Dr. Juris Tērauds, on the physical education faculty at the University of Maryland, developed a new theory and training method for javelin throwing. Tērauds analyzed the relationship between the force and the angle of thrust to the distance proving that the optimum angle is up to 10° smaller than previously thought (35° for a thrust velocity of 85-100 feet per sec.). Potentially, his method implies a radical increase in the record distances for this sport.

Jānis Egils Avots II, received a B.A. in the art of motion pictures at Brooks Institute in Santa Barbara, California. His short subject film Skylark and Me won first place at the Brooks film festival.

Father Leons Vārna was appointed coordinator of Latvian Catholic activities in the U.S.A. This position had been vacant since the death of Bishop Rancāns in 1969. Father Vārna is the head of the Latvian Catholic Congregation of Des Moines, Iowa.

Latvian artist Janis Gailis (born in Pērkone, Latvia in 1903) of New York, graduate of the Latvian Academy of Fine Arts, was commissioned by the 130-nation World Postal Federation to create a painting in honor of its founding in 1874. Gailis is known for his turbulent seascapes which have received numerous Latvian and international awards. His work Sails in the Wind will appear on the federation's limited issue of commemorative envelopes, scheduled to appear in March 1974.

Dr. Nina Podnieks, a general practitioner of dentistry in Falls Church, Virginia, graduate of the University of Latvia and the University of Pittsburgh Dental School, was one of six American women dentists chosen to exemplify her profession in the film Where I Want to be - the Story of a Woman Dentist. This film, part of an educational project sponsored by the U.S. Department of Health, Education, and Welfare, directed by Durrin Films, is intended for the promotion of professional careers among women.

Dr. R. Zemjānis, professor of reproductive biology at the School of Veterinary Medicine, University of Minnesota, received a U.S. Department of State appointment to Zaria, Nigeria, where he is to establish and head for two years a school of veterinary medicine at the Ahmad-Bello University. Zemjānis has served as a consultant for NASA and is an active member of the Latvian community in Minneapolis.

Mētra Pētersons, graduate of Drexel University and the
University of Maryland, became head librarian of the National Labor Relations Board in Washington, D.C.

Based on data from Latvian professional and academic organizations, the American Latvian Association reported the
approximate number of Latvian scholars and educators
serving on faculties of universities and other institutions
of higher learning throughout the United States to between
six hundred and seven hundred.

January 19. The Latvian Folk Dance Group of Grand Rapids,
Michigan performed at one of President Richard M. Nixon's
inaugural events in Washington, D.C. On January 20, the
Latvian Youth Folk Dance Group and the Youth Kokle En-
semble, directed by Mrs. Maija Ekšteins and Mr. Valdis
Kārklis, performed at the President's inaugural ball in the
Kennedy Center for the Performing Arts.

March 14. Rev. Jānis Siliņš, pastor of the Latvian Lutheran
Church of St. John since 1949, was the accidental victim of
a Philadelphia policeman's bullet, aimed at a fugitive criminal suspect fleeing across the church property. Rev. Siliņš
died twelve days later. On October 20, the church commemorated its eightieth anniversary.

April 13-15. A conference on the Baltic area in World War
II, organized by Dr. Edgar Andersons at Stanford University and California State University, San Jose, attracted
forty-two scholars from five countries and one hundred and
fifty general participants.

May. Dr. Jānis Auziņš of Michigan, a dentist in the U.S.
Army, was promoted to the rank of full colonel. At present
he is stationed at Fort Dix, New Jersey.

May. The twentieth annual competition in men's and women's volleyball and men's basketball was held in Washington, D.C. In this tournament the women's volleyball team
Sigulda of Washington, D.C., coached by Jānis Tērauds,
won its ninth award for the first place in Latvian women's
volleyball in the U.S.A. It was also the first time in Latvian sports history that a mother and two daughters, Ilze,

Silvija and Māra Pāža respectively, played simultaneously on the same team during the same game.

May 27. The tenth American Latvian Catholic Association Congress was held in Chicago. Father Baginskis of Chicago was elected to head the organization for a two-year period. The new president proposed the adaptation of Latvian folk melodies and texts for use during the mass.

June. Baltic demonstrations took place in Washington, D.C., Philadelphia, and New York during the visit of Leonid Brezhnev, secretary general of the Communist party of the U.S.S.R., to the United States.

June 29. Dr. Sigurds Krolls of the U.S. Air Force in Washington, D.C., was promoted from lieutenant colonel to the rank of full colonel. In addition to being one of the five most extensively educated men in oral pathalogy in the U.S. Air Force, he is also the first full colonel of Latvian descent to receive such a promotion in the U.S. Air Force.

July. The American Latvian Theatre of Washington, D.C., presented three performances of Bezkaunīgie veči by Anšlavs Eglītis to European audiences on the occasion of the Latvian Song Festival in Cologne, West Germany.

July 5. Uldis Grava, a citizen of the U.S.A., a marketing manager of the Newspaper Advertising Bureau in New York, was placed under arrest on unspecified charges by the Finnish police in Helsinki, Finland. At this time, the Conference on Security and Cooperation in Europe was taking place in Helsinki, attended by foreign ministers of numerous countries, including Secretary of State William Rogers of the U.S.A., and Foreign Minister Andrei Gromyko of the U.S.S.R. Concerned about the adverse effects this conference might have upon the future of the Soviet-occupied Baltic nations (Lithuania, Estonia and Latvia), the Baltic World Conference undertook to speak for their unrepresented countrymen. For this purpose, Grava and eight other Baltic leaders sought and were granted interviews with the accredited Western diplomats for discussions of the Baltic issue, introduced by memoranda and other supportive materials the Balts had submitted well in advance of the meeting. Demands of the U.S.S.R. that these Baltic activities be curtailed resulted in the incarceration of the Baltic representatives at the Espoo prison outside Helsinki. The course of

this incident evolved through several emergency sessions
of the Finnish cabinet, activated the official mechanisms
of the U.S. Department of State, and involved the personal
intervention of Secretary of State Rogers on behalf of the
arrested U.S. citizens. After a twenty-four-hour imprisonment, during which the Balts protested with a hunger strike,
they were released and the decision to deport them from
Finland cancelled. Any further political activity or contact
with the press was denied them, however. The Finnish
police demonstrably reluctant to perform the dictated arrests were now assigned to provide the Balts security and
protection against any attempts to intimidate them by the
Soviet agents, who had kept the Balts under constant sur-
veillance since their arrival.

September 17-22. Dr. Peter P. Lejins, director of the Institute of Criminal Justice and Criminology, took part in
the seventh International Congress on Criminology in Bel-
grade, Yugoslavia, convened by the International Society
for Criminology. Dr. Lejins acted as chairman of the coordinating group of the congress, in charge of synthesizing
the discussion and conclusions of the sessions on clinical
criminology, interactionist criminology and systems of
criminal justice.

October. The U.S. Department of the Interior selected the
New Seekers to represent musically the Clean up America
campaign in preparation for the nation's bicentennial. The
London-based pop group is known for its "We'd like to
Teach the World to Sing" best-seller. The official clean-up
song will be "We Gotta do it Now." A Latvian, Mārtiņš
Vanags, is a member of the New Seekers, where he is
known as Marty Kristian. Marty not only sings with them,
but is composer and lyricist for some of the New Seekers'
repertoire as well.

October 6-7. The first Latgallian culture days took place
in Toronto, Canada, with participation of distinguished Latgallian personalities from the U.S.A., including the Latvian
linguist Dr. Jāzeps Lelis of Washington, D.C., and novelist Jānis Klīdzējs of California. Latgallians, which are an
intrinsic part of the Latvian nation, posess a distinctive cultural and religious heritage, due to the history of Latgale,
which was for centuries politically separated from the rest
of Latvia.

November. Two milestone exhibits of Latvian art took
place in New York. August Annuss (born in 1893 in Liepāja,
Latvia), commemorated his eightieth birthday with a retrospective show of his works, ranging from a 1926 figurative
composition prepared for graduation from the Latvian Academy of Art, to his most recent symbolic works. Annuss
ranks as the Latvian master of figurative painting. He
taught at the Latvian Academy of Art; his works have appeared in every international exhibit where Latvians were
represented since 1936. In exile, he is also known for monumental altar pieces, depicting Christian themes in Latvian
settings and the refugee experience. Annus has served on
numerous judging and executive committees of major Latvian art events in the U.S.A., notably those connected with
folk festivals of the ALA's Culture Days. Anna Annus-Ha-
gen (born in 1937) and Jānis Annus (born in 1935), August
Annus' daughter and son respectively, a sculptress and a
painter, held a joint exhibit at the Central Arts Gallery in
Manhattan. This was a selected exhibit designed to show
each artist's characteristic and most accomplished works.
Both are graduates of the Pratt Institute in New York and
both are recipients of awards and international recognition.

November. A series of four one-half-hour television programs about Latvians were broadcast over KTCA 2, Minneapolis public television. Three of the programs were devoted respectively to Latvian history, Latvian music, and
Soviet oppression in Latvia. The concluding broadcast presented a Baltic panel of Estonian, Latvian, and Lithuanian
spokesmen, monitored by H. Wolf of KTCA, in a political
discussion of current East-West relationships. Aldona Pone
and Ēriks Dundurs were principal narrators for the series.

December. For the first time since 1949, a paper concerned
with Latvian history was on the agenda of the national conference of the American Historical Association. Dr. Andrejs Plakans (born in Latvia in 1940) presented "Peasant
Farms and Homesteads in the Baltic Littoral of 1797." Plakans, a graduate of Harvard, has received Fullbright, National Endowment for the Humanities, and other postdoctoral
grants for his innovative research of heretofore neglected
sociological and economic aspects of Latvian history prior
to the nineteenth century. Plakans is the first scholar to
utilize computers in the evaluation of data pertaining to Latvian history. At the same conference, Dr. Egils Grīslis
(born in Latvia in 1928), professor of religious studies and

philosophy at Hartford Seminary and subsequently at Fordham University, chaired a special seminar concerning rhetoric in the history of the Anglican Church.

Jānis Šāberts (born in 1892), a prominent actor of the Latvian stage, died in New York City.

Andrejs Karuliņš, known in Europe as the flamenco guitarist André el Letton, returned to his home town of Grand Rapids, Michigan. He gave a number of concerts for Latvian audiences in the U.S.A.

Document 1

LATVIAN DECLARATION OF INDEPENDENCE, 1918

Documents 1 and 2 represent the ideological foundation of the Latvian Republic; they are part of the heritage of the present Latvian-Americans.

(Source: "Waldibas Wehstnesis" December 14, 1918, No. 1 (Official Gazette). Bīlmanis, Alfred. Dr. comp. Latvian-Russian Relations. Washington, D.C.: The Latvian Legation, 1944, p. 59.)

The National Council of Latvia, deeming itself to be the only repository of the supreme power in the State of Latvia, declares, that:

1) Latvia, united in its ethnographic limits (Kurzeme, Vidzeme, and Latgale) -- is a self-governing, independent, democratic-republican State. (Its) Constitution and the relations with foreign states shall be specifically defined in the near future by a Constituent Assembly convoked on the basis of direct, general, equal, secret and proportional suffrage for both sexes.

2) The National Council of Latvia has established a Provisional Government of Latvia as the supreme executive power in Latvia.

The National Council of Latvia requests the citizens of Latvia to maintain peace and order and to assist the Provisional Government of Latvia with all their power in its difficult and responsible task.

Prime Minister of the Provisional Government of Latvia:

ULMANIS.

Deputy Chairman of the National Council of Latvia:

ZEMGALS.

Rīga, November 18, 1918.

Document 2

POLITICAL PLATFORM OF THE NATIONAL COUNCIL OF LATVIA
ADOPTED IN THE NOVEMBER 18, 1918 SESSION OF THE NATIONAL
COUNCIL OF LATVIA AT RIGA

(Source: Collection of Laws and Decrees of the Latvian Provisional Government, No. 2, July 15, 1919. Bilmanis, op. cit.,
pp. 59-60.)

I. CONSTITUENT ASSEMBLY

1) The Constituent Assembly of Latvia shall be convoked at the
earliest time possible.
2) Members of the Constituent Assembly shall be elected under the
participation of both sexes on the basis of general, equal, direct, secret
and proportional right to vote.

II. FORM OF STATE (ORGANIZATION) AND RELATIONS WITH OTHER
NATIONS

1) A republic based on democratic principles.
2) A united, self-governing and independent Latvia in the League of
Nations.

III. THE SOVEREIGN POWER AND THE POLITICAL AND ECONOMIC
ORGANIZATION OF THE STATE

1) Until the convocation of the Constituent Assembly, sovereign
power shall be vested in the National Council of Latvia, which shall also
appoint the Provisional Government.
2) The National Council of Latvia shall consist of the delegates of:
a) political parties, b) national minorities and c) those areas (novadi) of
Latvia, i.e. Kurzeme and Latgale, where there do not exist political
parties at the present moment.
3) In forming the Provisional Government the principle of coalition
shall be observed.
4) Until the (convocation of the) Constituent Assembly all executive
power shall vest in the Provisional Government.
5) Until the Constituent Assembly the Provisional Government has
no authority to change the existing social system.

IV. RIGHTS OF RACIAL MINORITIES (Zittauteeschu tiesibas)

1) National minorities shall delegate their representatives to the
Constituent Assembly and legislative agencies on the basis of the right
of proportional representation in the elections (see I, Para 2).

2) Those national minorities which are included in the National Council of Latvia, shall participate in the Provisional Government on the basis of Part III 3).

3) The cultural and national rights of national groups shall be ensured by the basic laws.

V. CIVIC LIBERTIES

1) Freedom of press, speech, assembly and association shall be ensured by regulations of the Provisional Government.

2) An amnesty (shall be granted) in all cases, except criminal cases.

3) A possibility for Latvian citizens to return to their homeland (shall be given).

VI. NATIONAL DEFENSE

1) The national militia of Latvia (defense force) shall be established on the basis of conscription, not excluding voluntary registration. The militia (national defense forces) shall be directly responsible to the Provisional Government organizing national defense.

2) The German army shall be evacuated within a definite period of time.

VII. MUNICIPALITIES

1) The election of Municipal Agencies shall take place on the basis of principles outlined in Part I, Para. 2. Prior to the Constituent Assembly, the Provisional Government shall fix the time for these elections and it shall also set up the provisional agencies of local administration.

Deputy Chairman of the National Council of Latvia:

ZEMGALS

Secretary:

BITTE

Document 3

RECOGNITION OF LATVIA BY THE UNITED STATES OF AMERICA
1922

The following document, along with Document 17, illustrates the relationships between Latvia and the United States at a time when the majority of Latvian-Americans were part of a thriving and peaceful population of the Republic of Latvia.

(Source: Collection of Laws and Decrees of the Latvian Provisional Government, No. 183. Also Bīlmanis, op. cit., pp. 66-67.)

860.n.01/52a: Telegram
The Secretary of State to the Commissioner at Riga (Young)
Washington, July 25, 1922, 4 p.m.
98 Advise Foreign Offices of Estonia, Latvia and Lithuania as nearly at the same time as possible on the morning of July 28, that the United States extend to each full recognition (Italics by the ref.). The fact will be communicated to the press at Washington for publication in the morning papers of July 28, and the following statement will be made:

"The Governments of Esthonia, Latvia and Lithuania have been recognized either de jure or de facto by the principal Governments of Europe and have entered into treaty relations with their neighbors.

"In extending to them recognition on its part, the Government of the United States takes cognizance of the actual existence of these Governments during a considerable period of time and the successful maintenance within their borders of political and economical stability.

"The United States has consistently maintained that the disturbed conditions of Russian affairs may not be made the occasion for alienation of Russian territory, and this principle is not deemed to be impinged by the recognition at this time of the Governments of Esthonia, Latvia and Lithuania which have been set up and maintained by an indigenous population. (Italics by the ref.).

"Pending legislation by Congress to establish regular diplomatic representation Mr. Young will continue as Commissioner of the United States and will have the rank of Minister. Request from respective Governments temporary recognition pending formal application for exequatures of John P. Hurley, Charles H. Albrecht, and Clement S. Edwards consuls at Riga, Reval and Kovno, respectively.

Signed: HUGHES.

Document 4

TREATY OF NONAGRESSION BETWEEN GERMANY AND THE UNION
OF SOVIET SOCIALIST REPUBLICS AND SECRET ADDITIONAL
PROTOCOL, 1939

The following item documents the historical and political reasons for the presence of a large segment of the Latvian population in the U.S. The first part of the treaty was made known to
the world. The second, pertaining to Latvia, remained a well-
kept secret until its discovery among Hitler's files.

(Source: U.S. Department of State. Nazi-Soviet Relations, 1939-
1941. Documents from the Archives of the German Foreign Office. Washington, D.C.: U.S. Government Printing Office, 1948,
pp. 76-78.)

TREATY OF NONAGGRESSION BETWEEN GERMANY AND THE UNION
OF SOVIET SOCIALIST REPUBLICS

The Government of the German Reich and
the Government of the Union of Soviet Socialist Republics
desirous of strengthening the cause of peace between Germany and
the U.S.S.R., and proceeding from the fundamental provisions of the
Neutrality Agreement concluded in April 1926 between Germany and the
U.S.S.R., have reached the following agreement:

ARTICLE I

Both High Contracting Parties obligate themselves to desist from
any act of violence, any aggressive action, and any attack of each other,
either individually or jointly with other powers.

ARTICLE II

Should one of the High Contracting Parties become the object of
belligerent action by a third power, the other High Contracting Party
shall in no manner lend its support to this third power.

ARTICLE III

The Governments of the two High Contracting Parties shall in the
future maintain continual contact with one another for the purpose of
consultation in order to exchange information on problems affecting their
common interests.

ARTICLE IV

Neither of the two High Contracting Parties shall participate in any grouping of powers whatsoever that is directly or indirectly aimed at the other party.

ARTICLE V

Should disputes or conflicts arise between the High Contracting Parties over problems of one kind or another, both parties shall settle these disputes or conflicts exclusively through friendly exchange of opinion or, if necessary, through the establishment of arbitration commissions.

ARTICLE VI

The present treaty is concluded for a period of ten years, with the proviso that, in so far as one of the High Contracting Parties does not denounce it one year prior to the expiration of this period, the validity of this treaty shall automatically be extended for another five years.

ARTICLE VII

The present treaty shall be ratified within the shortest possible time. The ratifications shall be exchanged in Berlin. The agreement shall enter into force as soon as it is signed.

Done in duplicate, in the German and Russian languages.

Moscow, August 23, 1939.

For the Government of the German Reich:	With full power of the Government of the U.S.S.R.:
v. RIBBENTROP	V. MOLOTOV

GERMAN-SOVIET SECRET PROTOCOL OF 1939 ON A DIVISION OF SPHERES OF INTEREST IN EASTERN EUROPE

(Source: Documents on German Foreign Policy 1918-1945, Series D (1937-1945), Vol. 7, Washington, D.C. 1956, pp. 246-247.)

Secret Additional Protocol

On the occasion of the signature of the Non-Aggression Treaty between the German Reich and the Union of Soviet Socialist Republics, the undersigned plenipotentiaries of the two Parties discussed in strictly confidential conversations the question of the delimitation of their respective spheres of interest in Eastern Europe. These conversations led to the following result:

1. In the event of a territorial and political transformation in the territories belonging to the Baltic States (Finland, Estonia, Latvia, Lithuania), the northern frontier of Lithuania shall represent the frontier of the spheres of interest both of Germany and the U.S.S.R. In this connection the interest of Lithuania in the Vilna territory is recognized by both Parties.

2. In the event of a territorial and political transformation of the territories belonging to the Polish State, the spheres of interest of both Germany and the U.S.S.R. shall be bounded approximately by the line of the rivers Narev, Vistula, and San.

The question whether the interests of both Parties make the maintenance of an independent Polish State appear desirable and how the frontiers of this State should be drawn can be definitely determined only in the course of further political developments.

In any case both Governments will resolve this question by means of a friendly understanding.

3. With regard to South-Eastern Europe, the Soviet side emphasizes its interest in Bessarabia. The German side declares complete political désintéressement in these territories.

4. This Protocol will be treated by both parties as strictly secret.

MOSCOW, August 23, 1939.

For the Government of
the German Reich:
v. RIBBENTROP

With full power of the
Government of the U.S.S.R:
V. MOLOTOV

Document 5

NKVD's ORDER OF 1939 REGARDING PROCEDURE OF DEPORTATIONS
IN LITHUANIA, LATVIA AND ESTONIA

Almost all Latvian-born Americans in this country today were historically threatened with the reality of the following outline of Soviet procedures. Members of families, relatives and close friends of the Latvian-born Americans in this country have been the victims of the Soviet deportations.

(Source: These Names Accuse: Nominal List of Latvians Deported to Soviet Russia in 1940-41. Stockholm: The Latvian National Fund in the Scandinavian Countries, 1951, pp. 41-48.)

ORDER No 001223

regarding the Procedure for carrying out the Deportation of Anti-Soviet Elements from Lithuania, Latvia, and Estonia.

STRICTLY SECRET.

(Translated from the Original Russian Text in London).

1. General Situation

The deportation of anti-Soviet elements from the Baltic Republics is a task of great political importance. Its successful execution depends upon the extent to which the district operative "troikas" and operative headquarters are capable of carefully working out a plan for executing the operations and for anticipating everything indispensable.

Moreover, care must be taken that the operations are carried out without disturbances and panic, so as not to permit any demonstrations and other troubles not only on the part of those to be deported, but also on the part of a certain section of the surrounding population hostile to the Soviet administration.

Instructions as to the procedure for conducting the operations are given below. They should be adhered to, but in individual cases the collaborators engaged in carrying out the operations shall take into account the special character of the concrete conditions of such operations and, in order to correctly appraise the situation, may and must adopt other decision directed to the same end, viz., to fulfil the task entrusted to them without noise and panic.

2. Procedure of Instructing

The instructing of operative groups by the district "troika" shall be done as speedily as possible on the day before the beginning of the operations, taking into consideration the time necessary for travelling to the scene of operations.

On the question of allocating the necessary number of motor-cars and waggons for transport, the district "troika" shall consult the leaders of the Soviet party organized on the spot.

Premises for the issue of instructions must be carefully prepared in advance, and their capacity, exits and entrances and the possibility of intrusion by strangers must be considered.

Whilst instructions are being issued the building must be carefully guarded by operative workers.

Should anybody from amongst those participating in the operation fail to appear for instructions, the district "troika" shall at once take steps to replace the absentee from a reserve which shall be provided in advance.

Through police officers the "troika" shall notify to those assembled a division of the government for the deportation of a prescribed number contingent of anti-Soviet elements from the territory of the said republic or region. Moreover, they shall briefly explain what the deportees represent.

The special attention of the (local) Soviet party workers gathered for instructions shall be drawn to the fact that the deportees are enemies of the Soviet people and that the possibility of an armed attack on the part of the deportees cannot be excluded.

3. Procedure for Acquisition of Documents

After the general instructions of the operative groups, documents regarding the deportees should be issued to such groups. The deportees' personal files must be previously collected and distributed among the operative groups, by communes and villages, so that when they are being given out there shall be no delays.

After receipt of personal files, the senior member of the operative group shall acquaint himself with the personal affairs of the families which he will have to deport. He shall, moreover, ascertain the composition of the family, the supply of essential forms for completion regarding the deportee, the supply of transport for conveyance of the deportee, and he shall receive exhaustive answers to questions not clear to him.

Simultaneously with the issuing of documents, the district "troika" shall explain to each senior member of the operative group where the families to be deported are situated and shall describe the route to be followed to the place of deportation. The roads to be taken by the operative personnel with the deported families to the railway station for entrainment shall be indicated. It is also essential to indicate where reserve military groups are stationed, should it be necessary to call them out during trouble of any kind.

The possession and state of arms and ammunition of the entire operative personnel shall be checked. Weapons must be in complete battle readiness and magazines loaded, but the cartridge shall not be slipped into the rifle breech. Weapons shall be used only as a last resort, when the operative group is attacked or threatened with attack or when resistance is offered.

4. Procedure for Carrying out Deportations

If the deportation of several families is being carried out in a settled locality, one of the operative workers shall be appointed senior as regards deportation in that village, and under his direction the operative personnel shall proceed to the villages in question. On arrival in the villages, the operative group shall get in touch (observing the necessary secrecy) with the local authorities: the chairman, secretary or members of the village soviets, and shall ascertain from them the exact dwelling-place of the families to be deported.

After this the operative groups, together with the representatives of the local authorities, who shall be appointed to make an inventory of property, shall proceed to the dwellings of the families to be deported. Operations shall be begun at daybreak. Upon entering the home of the person to be deported, the senior member of the operative group shall assemble the entire family of the deportee into one room, taking all necessary precautionary measures against any possible trouble.

After the members of the family have been checked in conformity with the list, the location of those absent and the number of sick persons shall be ascertained, after which they shall be called upon to give up their weapons. Irrespective of whether or not any weapons are delivered, the deportee shall be personally searched and then the entire premises shall be searched in order to discover hidden weapons.

During the search of the premises one of the members of the operative group shall be appointed to keep watch over the deportees.

Should the search disclose hidden weapons in small quantities, these shall be collected by the operative groups and distributied among them. If many weapons are discovered, they shall be piled into the wagon or motor-car which has brought the operative group, after any ammunition in them has been removed. Ammunition shall be packed together with rifles.

If necessary, a convoy for transporting the weapons shall be mobilized with an adequate guard.

In the event of the discovery of weapons, counter-revolutionary pamphlets, literature, foreign currency, large quantities of valuables etc., a brief report of search shall be drawn up on the spot, wherein the hidden weapons or counter-revolutionary literature shall be indicated. If there is any armed resistance, the question of the necessity of arresting the parties, showing such armed resistance, and of sending them to the district branch of the People's Commissariat of Public Security shall be decided by the district "troika."

A report shall be drawn up regarding the deportees in hiding or sick ones, and this report shall be signed by the representative of the Soviet party organization.

After completion of the search of the deportees they shall be notified that by a Government decision they will be deported to other regions of the Union.

The deportees shall be permitted to take with them household necessities not exceeding 100 kilograms in weight.

1. Suit. 2. Shoes. 3. Underwear. 4. Bedding. 5. Dishes. 6. Glass-

ware. 7. Kitchen-utensils. 8. Foods, an estimated month's supply for a family. 9. Money in their possession. 10. Trunk or box in which to pack articles. It is not recommended that large articles be taken.

If the contingent is deported from rural districts, they shall be allowed to take with them small agricultural stocks -- axes, saws, and other articles, so that when boarding the deportation train they may be loaded into special goods wagons.

In order not to mix them with articles belonging to others, the Christian name, patronymic and surname of the deportee and name of the village shall be written on the packed property.

When loading these articles into the carts, measures shall be taken so that the deportee cannot make use of them for purposes of resistance while the column is moving along the highway.

Simultaneously with the task of loading by the operative groups, the representatives of the Soviet party organizations present at the time prepare an inventory of the property and of the manner of its protection in conformity with the instructions received by them.

If the deportee possesses his own means of transport, his property shall be loaded into the vehicle and together with his family shall be sent to the designated place of entrainment.

If the deportees are without means of transport, carts shall be mobilized in the village by the local authorities, as instructed by the senior member of the operative group.

All persons entering the home of the deportee during the execution of the operations or found there at the moment of these operations must be detained until the conclusion of the operations, and their relationship to the deportee shall be ascertained. This is done in order to disclose persons hiding from the police, gendarmes and other persons. After verification of the identity of the detained persons and establishment of the fact that they are persons in whom the contingent is not interested they shall be liberated.

If the inhabitants of the village begin to gather around the deportees' home while operations are in progress, they shall be called upon to disperse to their own homes, and crowds shall not be permitted to form. If the deportee refuses to open the door of his home, notwithstanding that he is aware that the members of the People's Commissariat for Public Security have arrived, the door must be broken down. In individual cases neighbouring operative groups carrying out operations in that locality shall be called upon to help.

The delivery of the deportees from the village to the meeting place at the railway station must be effected during daylight; care, moreover, should be taken that the assembling of every family shall not last more than two hours.

In all cases throughout the operations firm and decisive action shall be taken, without the slightest excitement, noise and panic.

It is categorically forbidden to take any articles away from the deportees except weapons, counter-revolutionary literature and foreign currency, as also to make use of the food of the deportees.

All participants in the operations must be warned that they will be held legally accountable for attempts to appropriate individual articles belonging to the deportees.

5. Procedure for Separating a Deportee's Family from the Head of the Family.

In view of the fact that a large number of deportees must be arrested and distributed in special camps and that their families must proceed to special settlements in distant regions, it is essential that the operations of removal of both the members of the deportee's family and its head shall be carried out simultaneously, without notifying them of the separation confronting them. After the domiciliary search has been carried out and the appropriate identification documents have been drawn up in the deportee's home, the operative worker shall complete the documents for the head of the family and deposit them in the latter's personal file, but the documents drawn up for members of his family shall be deposited in the personal file of the deportee's family. The convoy of the entire family to the station shall, however, be effected in one vehicle and only at the station of departure shall the head of the family be placed separately from his family in a car specially intended for heads of families.

During the assembling (of the family) in the home of the deportee the head of the family shall be warned that personal male effects must be packed in a separate suitcase, as a sanitary inspection of the deported men will be made separately from the women and children.

At the stations of entrainment heads of families subject to arrest shall be loaded into cars specially allotted to them, which shall be indicated by operative workers appointed for that purpose.

6. Procedure for convoying the Deportees

The assistans convoying the column of deportees in horse-carts are strictly forbidden to sit in the said carts. The assistants must follow alongside and behind the column of deportees. The senior assistant of the convoy shall from time of time go the rounds of the entire column to check the correctness of the movement.

When the column of the deportees is passing through inhabited places or when encountering passers-by, the convoy must be controlled with particular care; those in charge must see that no attempts are made to escape, and no conversation of any kind shall be permitted between the deportees and passers-by.

7. Procedure for Entrainment.

At each point of entrainment a member of the operative "troika" and a person specially appointed for that purpose shall be responsible for entrainment.

On the day of entrainment the chief of the entrainment point, together with the chief of the deportation train and of the convoying military forces of the People's Commissariat of Internal Affairs, shall examine the railway cars provided in order to see that they are supplied with everything necessary, and the chief of the entrainment point shall agree with the chief of the deportation train on the procedure to be observed by the latter in accepting delivery of the deportees.

Red Army men of the convoying forces of the People's Commissariat of Internal Affairs shall surround the entrainment station.

The senior members of the operative group shall deliver to the chief of the deportation train one copy of the nominal roll of the deportees in each railway-car. The chief of the deportation train shall, in conformity with this list, call out the name of each deportee, shall carefully check every name and assign the deportee's place in the railway-car.

The deportee's effects shall be loaded into the car, together with the deportee, with the exception of the small agricultural inventory, which shall be loaded in a separate car.

The deportees shall be loaded into railway-cars by families; it is permitted to break up a family (with the exception of heads of families subject to arrest). An estimate of twenty-five persons to a car should be observed.

After the railway-car has been filled with the necessary number of families, it shall be locked.

After the people have been taken over and placed in the deportation train, the chief of the train shall bear responsibility for all persons handed over to him and for their delivery to their destination. After handing over the deportees the senior member of the operative group shall draw up a report on the operation carried out by him and briefly indicate the name of the deportee, whether any weapon and counter-revolutionary literature have been discovered, and also how the operation was carried out.

After having placed the deportees on the deportation train and having submitted reports of the results of the operations to be thus discharged, the members of the operative group shall be considered free and shall act in accordance with the instructions of the chief of the district branch of the People's Commissariat of Public Security.

Deputy People's Commissar of Public Security of the USSR. Commissar of Public Security of the third Rank (signed):

SEROV.

Document 6

LETTER FROM SUMNER WELLES TO DR. ALFRED BILMANIS,
1941

> To Latvians in the United States this docu-
> ment, along with Documents 7, 9, 11 and
> 15, is of importance.

DEPARTMENT OF STATE
WASHINGTON

November 15, 1941.

Sir:

I have the honor to acknowledge the receipt of your note of November
21, 1941 transmitting a copy of a communication dated August 30, 1941 from
the Latvian Minister at London to His Majesty's Principal Secretary of
State for Foreign Affairs, in which it is stated that the legal existence of
the Latvian Republic can in no way be affected by the change in Latvia
from Soviet military occupation to German military occupation.

In this connection it is of interest to recall that in the joint declaration
agreed upon by the President of the United States and the Prime Minister of
Great Britain during their historic meeting at sea it is stated that the United
States and Great Britain respect the right of all peoples to choose the form
of government under which they desire to live and that the United States
and Great Britain wish to see self-government restored to those peoples
who have been forcibly deprived of it.

Accept, Sir, the renewed assurances of my highest consideration.

For the Secretary of State:

/-/ Sumner Welles.

The Honorable
    Dr. Alfred Bilmanis
        Minister of Latvia.

Document 7

U.S. REFUSAL TO RECOGNIZE ACTS OF SOVIET REGIME
IN LATVIA, 1940

No. 5235
United States of America
Department of State

To all to whom these presents shall come, Greeting:

I Certify That the legality of the so-called "nationalization" laws and decrees, or of any of the acts of the Soviet regime which assumed power in Latvia in 1940, or of any subsequent regime in that country has not been recognized by the Government of the United States.

In testimony whereof, I, GEORGE C. MARSHALL,
Secretary of State, have hereunto caused the seal of the Department of State to be affixed and my name subscribed by the Authentication Officer of the said Department, at the City of Washington, in the District of Columbia, this   twenty-eighth
day of   May   , 1942.

GEORGE C. MARSHALL
Secretary of State

By M. P. Chauvin
Authentication Officer, Department
of State.

Document 8

EXISTENCE OF U.S.-LATVIAN TREATIES NOT AFFECTED
BY ACTS OF SOVIET REGIME, 1947

For such U.S. treaties with Latvia as are in
force presently, please consult U.S. Depart-
ment of State. Treaties in Force: A List of
Treaties and Other International Agreements
of the United States in Force on January 1, 1973.
Washington, D.C.: U.S. Government Printing
Office, 1973, p. 151. Department of State
Publication 8697.

No. 5233
United States of America
Department of State

To all to whom these presents shall come, Greeting:

I Certify That the legal existence of the Treaty of Friendship, Commerce and Consular Rights, as well as of all other treaties between the
United States and the Republic of Latvia has not been affected by any of the
acts of the Soviet regime which assumed power in Latvia in 1940, or of any
subsequent regime in that country.

In testimony whereof, I, GEORGE C. MARSHALL,
Secretary of State, have hereunto caused the seal of
the Department of State to be affixed and my name
subscribed by the Authentication Officer of the said
Department, at the city of Washington, in the District of Columbia, this twenty-eighth
day of   May   ,   1947.

(signed)   GEORGE C. MARSHALL
Secretary of State

(signed) By M.P. CHAUVIN
Authentication Officer, Department of State

Document 9

U.S. REFUSAL TO RECOGNIZE INCORPORATION
OF LATVIA INTO U.S.S.R., 1947

No. 5234

United States of America
Department of State

To whom these presents shall come, Greeting:

I Certify That the incorporation of Latvia by the Union of Soviet
Socialist Republics is not recognized by the Government of the United
States.

In testimony whereof, I, GEORGE C. MARSHALL,
Secretary of State have hereunto caused the seal of the
Department of State to be affixed and my name subscribed
by the Authentication Officer of the said Department, at
the city of Washington, in the District of Columbia,
this,   twenty-eighth
day of   May   , 1947.

(signed)   GEORGE C. MARSHALL
Secretary of State

(signed) By   M. P. CHAUVIN
Authentication Officer,
Department of State

Document 10

DR. KARLIS ULMANIS MEMORIAL PLAQUE, 1954

Latvian Americans are proud of the historical link
between the United States and Latvia which has been
established by one of their most distinguished statesmen, Karlis Ulmanis. The following inscription
appears on the memorial plaque dedicated by the
Latvian Press Society in 1954 at the University of
Nebraska at Lincoln.

DR. KARLIS ULMANIS

BORN IN LATVIA ON SEPTEMBER 4, 1877, FIRST
PRIME MINISTER AND LATER PRESIDENT OF THE
INDEPENDENT LATVIAN REPUBLIC, RECEIVED HIS
          B.S. AT THIS UNIVERSITY IN 1909.
AFTER THE ILLEGAL SOVIET OCCUPATION OF
LATVIA IN 1940, THIS GREAT LATVIAN PATRIOT
AND LIFELONG FRIEND OF THE UNITED STATES
WAS DEPORTED TO SOVIET RUSSIA, WITH MA-
NY THOUSANDS OF OTHER LATVIAN CITIZENS
WHO WERE PLACED IN FORCED LABOR CAMPS.
THE SUBSEQUENT FATE OF PRESIDENT ULMANIS
          IS UNKNOWN.
THIS MEMORIAL PLAQUE HAS BEEN DEDICATED
BY THE LATVIAN PRESS SOCIETY IN AMERICA WITH
THE SUPPORT OF VOLUNTARY DONATIONS.   1954

DR. KĀRLIS ULMANIS,
DZIMIS LATVIJĀ, 1877. GADA 4. SEPTEMBRĪ,
NEATKARĪGĀS LATVIJAS REPUBLIKAS PIRMAIS
MINISTRU UN VĒLĀK VALSTS PREZIDENTS, IEGU-
VA ŠINĪ UNIVERSITĀTĒ ZINĀTŅU BAKALAURA GRĀ-
          DU 1909. GADĀ.
PADOMJU SAVIENĪBAI 1940. GADĀ NELIKUMĪGI
OKUPĒJOT LATVIJU, ŠO LIELO LATVIEŠU PATRIO-
TU UN UZTICĪGO AMERIKAS SAVIENOTO VALSTU
DRAUGU AIZVEDA UZ PADOMJU SAVIENĪBU, LĪDZ
AR DAUDZ TŪKSTOŠIEM LATVIJAS PILSOŅU, KU-
ŖUS IEVIETOJA VERGU DARBA NOMETNĒS. PAR
      PREZIDENTA ULMAŅA LIKTENI ZIŅU NAV.
ŠO PIEMIŅAS PLAKSNI AŖ SABIEDRĪBAS ATBALSTU
UZSTĀDĪJA LATVIEŠU PRESES BIEDRĪBA.

Document 11

CAPTIVE NATIONS WEEK, 1959 -- A PROCLAMATION BY THE PRESIDENT OF THE UNITED STATES OF AMERICA

Source: 91st Congress.   House.   Forward-Looking Addresses in the House of Representatives together with Documents on the Captive Nations Week Movement. Washington, D.C. U.S. Government Printing Office, 1969, p. 3 (House Document No. 91-184)

Whereas many nations throught the world have been made captive by the imperialistic and aggressive policies of Soviet communism; and

Whereas the citizens of the United States are linked by bonds of family and principle to those who love freedom and justice on every continent; and

Whereas it is appropriate and proper to manifest to the peoples of the captive nations the support of the Government and the people of the United States of America for their just aspirations for freedom and national independence; and

Whereas by a joint resolution approved July 17, 1959, the Congress has authorized and requested the President of the United States of America to issue a proclamation designating the third week in July, 1959, as "Captive Nations Week," and to issue a similar proclamation each year until such time as freedom and independence shall have been achieved for all the captive nations of the world:

Now, therefore, I, Dwight D. Eisenhower, President of the United States of America, do hereby designate the week beginning July 19, 1959, as Captive Nations Week.

I invite the people of the United States of America to observe such week with appropriate ceremonies and activities, and I urge them to study the plight of the Soviet-dominated nations and to recommit themselves to the support of the just aspirations of the peoples of those captive nations.

In witness whereof, I have hereunto set my hand and caused the Seal of the United States of America to be affixed.

Done at the city of Washington this 17th day of July in the year of our Lord 1959, and of the independence of the United States of America the 184th.

By the President:

Seal   DWIGHT D. EISENHOWER
                                  CHRISTIAN A. HERTER,
                                  Secretary of State.

Document 12

PUBLIC LAW 86-90: CAPTIVE NATIONS WEEK
RESOLUTION, 1959

Source: 91st Congress. House. Forward-Looking Addresses in the House
of Representatives together with Documents on the Captive Nations Week
Movement. Washington, D.C.: U.S. Government Printing Office, 1969,
pp. 1-2. (House Document No. 91-184).

JOINT RESOLUTION Providing for the designation of the third week of July
as "Captive Nations Week"

Whereas the greatness of the United States is in large part attributable
to its having been able, through the democratic process, to achieve a harmonious national unity of its people, even though they stem from the most
diverse of racial, religious, and ethnic backgrounds; and

Whereas this harmonious unification of the diverse elements of our
free society has led the people of the United States to possess a warm understanding and sympathy for the aspirations of peoples everywhere and to
recognize the natural interdependency of the peoples and nations of the
world; and

Whereas the enslavement of a substantial part of the world's population
by Communist imperialism makes a mockery of the idea of peaceful coex-
istence between nations and constitutes a detriment to the natural bonds of
understanding between the people of the United States and other peoples; and

Whereas since 1918 the imperialistic and aggressive policies of Russian
Communism have resulted in the creation of a vast empire which poses a
dire threat to the security of the United States and of all the free peoples of
the world; and

Whereas the imperialistic policies of Communist Russia have led,
through direct and indirect aggression, to the subjugation of the national independence of Poland, Hungary, Lithuania, Ukraine, Czechoslovakia, Latvia, Estonia, White Ruthenia, Rumania, East Germany, Bulgaria, mainland
China, Armenia, Azerbaijan, Georgia, North Korea, Albania, Idel-Ural,
Tibet, Cossackia, Turkestan, North Viet-Nam, and others; and

Whereas these submerged nations look to the United States, as the cit-
adel of human freedom, for leadership in bringing about their liberation
and independence and in restoring to them the enjoyment of their Christian,
Jewish, Moslem, Buddhist, or other religious freedoms, and of their individual liberties; and

Whereas it is vital to the national security of the United States that the
desire for liberty and independence on the part of the peoples of these con-
quered nations should be steadfastly kept alive; and

Whereas the desire for liberty and independence by the overwhelming majority of the people of these submerged nations constitutes a powerful deterrent to war and one of the best hopes for a just and lasting peace; and

Whereas it is fitting that we clearly manifest to such peoples through an appropriate and official means the historic fact that the people of the United States share with them their aspirations for the recovery of their freedom and independence: Now, therefore, be it

Resolved by the Senate and House of Representatives of the United States of America in Congress assembled, That the President of the United States is authorized and requested to issue a proclamation designating the third week in July 1959 as "Captive Nations Week" and inviting the people of the United States to observe such week with appropriate ceremonies and activities. The President is further authorized and requested to issue a similar proclamation each year until such time as freedom and independence shall have been achieved for all the captive nations of the world.

Approved July 17, 1959.

Document 13

LETTER FROM SECRETARY OF STATE ROGERS TO DR. ANATOL DINBERGS, 1972

THE SECRETARY OF STATE
Washington

November 6, 1972

Dear Mr. Charge d'Affaires:

On behalf of the Government and people of the United States, I wish to extend to you greetings and sincere good wishes in connection with the fifty-fourth anniversary of the proclamation of Latvian independence, which will be celebrated on November 18.

Although Latvian independence was repressed in 1940, the people of Latvia have continued to manifest their indomitable national spirit. They have not ceased to hope that once again they will achieve the right to self-determination, a hope that is shared by the people of the United States and free peoples everywhere.

The United States, which has greatly benefitted from the contributions made by many Latvians to its national life, continues to support the Latvian people in their efforts to achieve a free and independent national existence in their homeland.

Sincerely, (signed)

WILLIAM P. ROGERS

Dr. Anatol Dinbergs,
Charge d'Affaires of Latvia.

Document 14

PRESIDENTIAL APPOINTMENT OF DR. PETER LEJINS AS U.S. REP-
RESENTATIVE TO THE U.N. PROGRAM FOR THE PREVENTION OF
CRIME AND THE TREATMENT OF OFFENDERS, 1972

Dr. Lejins' presidential appointment is among the highest
honors and responsibilities earned by an individual of Latvian
descent in this country. Less distinguished, but equally competent
and vital are the roles of individual Latvians in many relevant
aspects of American life.

THE WHITE HOUSE
Washington

July 28, 1972

Dear Dr. Lejins:

It is a pleasure to appoint you Representative of the United States to
participate, as a national correspondent, in the United Nations Program
for the Prevention of Crime and the Treatment of Offenders for a term
expiring December 31, 1975.

In this capacity, you will keep the Secretary General of the United Nations
informed of current developments in the United States in matters pertaining
to the prevention of crime and the treatment of offenders.

This appointment is made in accordance with resolution 415 (V) of
December 1, 1950 of the General Assembly of the United Nations which
provides for the appointment of national correspondents by member
governments.

Sincerely, (signed)

RICHARD NIXON

The Honorable Peter P. Lejins
Professor Sociology
Director
Institute of Criminal Justice and Criminology
University of Maryland
College Park, Maryland

Document 15

DETENTION OF AMERICANS OF BALTIC DESCENT DURING THE
EUROPEAN SECURITY CONFERENCE, 1973

The recent minor international incident described in the Congressional Record is considered as an important occurrence by Latvians in the free world.

(Source: Congressional Record -- Senate, September 5, 1973, S15877 - S15879.)

DETENTION OF AMERICANS OF BALTIC DESCENT IN HELSINKI, FINLAND, DURING THE EUROPEAN SECURITY CONFERENCE.

Mr. BUCKLEY. Mr. President, increasing concern has been expressed here and in Europe over the possibility that the Soviet Union is engaged in a massive diplomatic offensive designed to consolidate its hegemony over Eastern Europe while disrupting the move toward unity with the NATO and Common Market nations. The Soviet's ultimate objective is toward the "Finlandization" of Europe. This would be brought about when in the face of overwhelming Russian military strength, and of their own disunity, the nations of Western Europe one by one seek an accommodation with the Soviet Union.

An example of what is to be "Finlandization" was recently brought to my attention when five Americans of Baltic extraction were tossed into jail by Finnish authorities at the request of the Soviet delegation to the recent Helsinki Conference on European Security and Cooperation. Their offense? One of them annoyed Andrei Gromyko with a question at a press reception.

Mr. President, I ask unanimous consent that there be printed in the RECORD a copy of a memorandum describing the incident prepared by Dr. Joseph K. Valiunas, one of the Americans who was involved. I also ask unanimous consent that a report I received from the American Ambassador to Finland also be printed in the RECORD.

There being no objection, the statement and report were ordered to be printed in the RECORD, as follows:

Statement on the Activities and Dentention of Americans of Baltic Descent
in Helsinki, Finland, During the European Security Conference

Most Western observers will concur that the Soviet Bloc and the West confronted each other in Helsinki during the 35-nation European Security Conference. The key controversy was over the freer movement of men and ideas. The arrest and brief detention of nine spokesmen of the Baltic World Conference dramatically demonstrated that the Soviet interpretation of European cooperation remained worlds apart from the views of the Western countries. The nine Balts were arrested upon the explicit demand by the Soviet Delegation.

Permit me to recapitulate the events that led up to and followed the arrest by Finnish authorities of the delegation sent by the Baltic World Conference to Helsinki, Finland.

The Baltic World Conference was established in 1972 in New York City for the express purpose of coordinating the activities of Estonian, Latvian, and Lithuanian political and civic institutions dedicated to the restoration of national sovereignty and political freedoms to the Baltic States, currently under Soviet domination. The three major groupings which form the basis of the Baltic World Conference are the Supreme Committee for Liberation of Lithuania, the World Federation of Free Latvians, and the Estonian National Council.

The Baltic World Conference sent a nine-man delegation to the European Security Conference. The delegation consisted of the following persons:

1. Dr. Joseph K. Valiunas, President of the Baltic World Conference and President of the Supreme Committee for Liberation of Lithuania, (U.S. citizen);

2. Uldis Grava, President of the World Federation of Free Latvians (U.S. citizen);

3. Ilmas Pleer, V. President of the Estonian-American National Council, (U.S. citizen);

4. Georg Kahar, Estonian Central Council in Canada, (Canadian citizen);

5. Pauls Reinhards, President of the Latvian European Committe, (subject of Great Britain);

6. Dr. Aina Teivens, Latvian Council in Sweden, (subject of Sweden);

7. Egle Zilionis, Delegate of Baltic World Conference, (U.S. citizen);

8. Dr. Petras Vileisis, Representative of the Lithuanian Community of the USA, (U.S. citizen);

9. Dr. John Genys, Representative of the Lithuanian-American Council, (U.S. citizen).

The purpose of the Baltic mission was to present the Baltic case to the diplomats and journalists attending the Conference. This was to be attained by distributing information kits to the delegations and media, and by conferring personally with diplomats and journalists. The information kits contained a joint note drafted by the three Baltic delegations, an abbreviated version of a memorandum, submitted to the European Governments last November by the Supreme Committee for Liberation of Lithuania, and an invitation to a Baltic press conference planned for the 6th of July. Each national delegation also brought literature of an informative and legalistic nature, describing the present situation in Estonia, Latvia, and Lithuania.

None of the literature was of an inflammatory or demagogical nature. For example, the one-page memorandum of the Supreme Committee for Liberation of Lithuania focused on the following salient point:

"The European Conference on Security and Cooperation represents Moscow's latest attempt to obtain international legalization of its annexation of Lithuania, Latvia, and Estonia. Today the attempt is cloaked with such phrases as 'normalization of the situation in Europe,' and 'territorial

integrity of the states and inviolability of their frontiers.' Should the
Western Powers accept the above formulae without duly qualifying them,
the Soviet Government would interpret them as Western acquiescence
in Soviet annexation.''

In a word, the three Baltic delegations acting in unison attempted
to convey the thought that the Western countries should use the European
Conference as an opportunity to insist that the Government of the USSR
honor its prewar commitments and pledges by withdrawing its armed
forces and administrative apparatus from Estonia, Latvia, and Lithuania.

Arriving between July 1 and 4th, the nine Baltic spokesmen sojourned
at the Inter-Continental Hotel, which housed most of the diplomats to
the Conference. Three Latvians and one Lithuanian had valid credentials
as newspaper representatives. This permitted them to enter the press
gallery and observe the Conference in session. The others availed themselves of the opportunity to confer with newspeople and members of the
delegations in the antechambers during recess.

On July 4th, forming four operational groups, the Balts visited
most diplomatic delegations and embassies, at which time they submitted their information kits and memoranda. The contacts were formal and
protocol was observed. The following day Miss Zilionis and Dr. Teivens
distributed similar kits to the four hundred journalists and media people.
It is not true that the Balts disseminated leaflets in Finnish in front of
Finlandia Symphony Hall or at the entrance of the Inter-Continental Hotel.
No scenes of disturbance occurred. All meetings were tactful. For
example, Dr. Petras Vileisis went so far as to arrange a dinner engagement
with the Canadian Secretary for External Affairs.

The efforts of the Baltic World Conference were thwarted as a
result of a passing incident during the press reception held at the East
German Embassy. On the evening of July 4th, Mr. Uldis Grava, Chairman
of the Latvian contingent, was invited and attended the reception. In the
course of the evening, he approached Sir Alec Douglas-Home, British
Foreign Minister, and asked the latter why there were no diplomats of
the three Baltic Republics at the Conference. Sir Alec allegedly replied:
''Why do you ask me? Why don't you ask my colleague, Mr. Gromyko of
the Soviet Union?'' At first Mr. Andrei Gromyko mistook Mr. Grava for
an underling of the USSR. Mr. Grava calmly, but in a loud voice, asked
Mr. Andrei Gromyko why the Baltic question was not on the agenda. He
explained that he represented the Baltic World Conference which was
demanding freedom for Estonia, Latvia, and Lithuania. Seeing that
Mr. Gromyko was evasive, he reiterated the statement: ''The Baltic
States must have full freedom.'' A number of guests were attracted by this
dialogue. Whereupon Mr. Gromyko emphatically denied that the Soviet Union
had forcibly occupied the Baltic States and submitted Mr. Grava to verbal
abuse. He concluded his heated remarks in garbled English with the words:
''The Baltic countries voluntarily joined the Soviet Union, and the Baltic
States do not need any other freedoms!'' Mr. Gromyko abruptly turned
heel and stalked away.

Upon the request of the other Soviet officials, two East German
security agents asked Mr. Grava to leave. He did so without incident.
This brief tete-a-tete brought down the wrath of the Soviets upon the

Baltic mission. The Soviet Delegation did not waste any time in drafting
a stern note to the Finnish Government demanding the immediate arrest of the Balts. In other words, the Soviets had the audacity to order
a sovereign state to detain citizens of friendly powers because the latters'
views were embarrassing to Moscow. And this was done during a conference devoted to international cooperation. It was a saddening experience
to see the Finns submit to this diplomatic brow-beating.

On the morning of July 5th, Mr. Grava was arrested with Dr. Valiunas,
the chairman. At approximately 10:30 a.m. three Finnish plainclothesmen
knocked on his door, stating that they had a few questions. Upon entering,
they noticed the piles of Baltic literature in the room. Dr. Valiumas
permitted them to take samples. They did so and promptly informed the
three Balts that they are under arrest. The threesome was conducted to
a room where the Finnish security police had a stakeout to observe the
hotel guests.

The officer in charge asked Dr. Valiunas why the Balts had come to
the Conference. Dr. Valiunas countered with a question of his own: "Who
made the decision to arrest the Balts? The Finnish Ministry of the Interior or the Ministry of Foreign Affairs?" The reply was: the Interior.
Dr. Valiunas asked that he be permitted to inform the Finnish Foreign
Ministry and the American Embassy about the arrests.

The arrested Balts were led out to Police Headquarters. In the
hotel corridor, Dr. Valiunas bumped into Dr. Genys, who was still free.
He asked in Lithuanian to inform Lithuanian circles in the United States
that the three Baltic chairmen were arrested. Dr. Genys complied. He
also chanced to meet Dr. Vileisis who was asked to inform Mr. J. Audenas
of the Supreme Committee for Liberation of Lithuania about this development.

When the officers accompanying the Balts to Police Headquarters were
asked why they were arrested, the reply was vague. The arresting
officers stated that they did not know the reason. At Headquarters, Valiunas,
Grava, Pleer and Kahar agreed to admit the truth about the Baltic World
Conference's purpose in Helsinki because there was nothing to hide. They
were interrogated individually by the Commissioner of Police. Within
a short time, Mr. Terry Dale Hansen, Second Secretary to the U.S. Embassy
in Helsinki, arrived on the scene to witness the questioning.

That same day, July 5th, the other five Balts were arrested. Dr.
Vileisis was the last to be detained by the Finnish police and put in jail.

The interrogators asked if the Balts had distributed literature near
the Finlandia Symphony Hall or by the entrance to the Inter-Continental
Hotel. The reply was negative. The Balts explained that information kits
had been personally distributed to the journalists and diplomats in the
name of the Baltic World Conference. The Finnish Police Commissioner
asked in what manner did the Foreign Ministers receive the material.
The Balts answered that personal visits were made to each Embassy. It
should be kept in mind, that at no time did the Commissioner state the
reason for the arrests. He did not make any formal charges. However,
he hinted that the length of detention was still indeterminate.

The Police Commissioner requested Dr. Valiunas, as President of the
Baltic World Conference, to sign the statement of testimony recorded by

the police. When the latter refused, arguing that he did not read Finnish and that it was unjust to try to force a man to sign a statement in a language unknown to him, the statement was signed by the Commissioner and the interpreter.

Thereupon the arrested Balts were informed that they would be conveyed to prison. They were permitted to take personal effects from their hotel rooms for overnight use. Eight of the arrestees were taken to a prison in the suburbs of Helsinki. The prison officials confiscated the neckties, belts and shoelaces of the men, as was the procedure with convicts admitted.

The eight internees decided to go on a hunger strike as a sign of protest for this unfair internment without formal accusation. It must be remembered that they had not eaten since their apprehension. Each prisoner was locked in a narrow cement cell in solitary confinement. Their feelings were mixed with anxiety to say the least.

Unbeknownst to the arrestees, Estonian, Latvian and Lithuanian civic groups in the United States took action to secure the release of the nine. Senator James Buckley of New York and Congressman Edward Derwinski of Illinois contacted the White House and the State Department to ascertain the details of these arrests. Thanks to their efforts, Secretary of State William P. Rogers and Ambassador John Krehbiel were cabled to intercede. Upon learning of the arrests, Secretary Rogers telephoned the Finnish Foreign Ministry and secured the promise that the U.S. citizens would be released.

At dawn, on July 6th, prison officials roused the eight arrestees and informed them that the American citizens could go to Hotel Marswy. When it was learned that their English, Swedish and Canadian colleagues were to remain in prison, the American citizens declared their moral solidarity with the other three, declaring that all eight were to go or no one would leave. This impressed the prison officials. About 8 a.m. all eight were taken to a hotel near the prison. They were offered a lavish breakfast, which was paid for by the Finnish guards who sympathized with them. However, the Balts refused to breakfast, maintaining their hunger strike until they were released. While at this hotel they were kept incommunicado before being brought back to prison.

In the end, the Police Commissioner appeared and informed them that they were free, but that they could not hold the press conference which was scheduled for the sixth, nor could they engage in "any political activities." Furthermore, their press credentials were voided and the reservations at the Inter-Continental Hotel were canceled. Thereupon they were taken to Hotel Marsky where they joined Dr. Vileisis who had been kept under false arrest and incommunicado at that hotel.

The parting gesture of the Balts took place on Sunday, July 8th. The representatives of the Baltic World Conference went to the Finnish Cemetery of Heroes and placed flowers with Finnish national colors on the monument of Marshal Mannerheim. This gesture had a positive effect on the Finns who observed this modest ceremony. At departure time, that afternoon, a high police official pressed Dr. Valiunas' hand and stated: "Mr. President, I apologize for what has happened. This was not the true sentiment of the Finnish people toward your cause. Please believe me!"

In conclusion, the representatives of the World Baltic Conference do not bear any malice toward the Finnish authorities. The fact of the matter is, that the Soviet Delegation disdained being reminded of the grim reality of the illegal Soviet occupation of Estonia, Latvia, and Lithuania. As a result, Finnish authorities were forced to heed the displeasure of their powerful neighbor, the Soviet Union. In evaluating the outcome of this first European Security Conference, one should reflect that the detention of six Americans and three Westerners of Baltic descent in Helsinki conflicts with the avowed American goal of a European continent open to the free flow of ideas and people.

New York, July 12, 1973.

Joseph K. Valiunas,
President, Supreme Committee for Liberation
of Lithuania

AMERICAN EMBASSY
Helsinki, Finland, July 6, 1973.
ARREST REPORT

The Finnish government was extremely conscious of security problems and possible political activity by ethnic groups during the Conference on Security and Cooperation in Europe because of the large number of important officials present. Of particular concern to Finnish authorities was the possibility of demonstrations or similar activites which might disrupt the Conference. As a result of this sensitivity, the Finnish police took into custody on July 5 six American citizens who they believed intended to distribute at the Conference copies of a memorandum setting forth their opposition to the incorporation of the Baltic states into the Soviet Union. Five of the Americans were members of the Baltic World Conference, a U.S.-based group advocating the independence of Lithuania, Latvia, and Estonia. In addition to the Americans, three other persons (Swedish, Canadian, and British) were taken into custody. The Finnish police informed the Embassy that the Americans were not under arrest and had not been charged with a crime, but were being held for questioning, a normal procedure under Finnish law.

An Embassy officer proceeded to the Helsinki police headquarters and interviewed the Americans involved. They explained that they had not intended to disrupt the Conference in any way, but considered it an appropriate forum for the presentation of their views. They said that they had sent copies of their memorandum to the Foreign Ministers present at the Conference and had discussed their views with some of the Ministers or their representatives. They planned to hold a press conference on July 6 to answer questions on the current status of the Baltic states and the historical background of their incorporation into the U.S.S.R. They also planned to give to the press copies of their memorandum. They said that they had not intended to distribute their memorandum to the general public, but one member of the group had given two copies to Finnish plainclothes security officers at the Hotel Intercontinental, where the

American group, as well as many of the delegates, was staying.

Upon learning of the detention of the Americans, Secretary of State Rogers, who was representing the United States at the Conference, personally indicated to the Finnish government his concern about their detention and welfare. The Finnish Government agreed at once to their release, and they were freed the morning of July 6. The only limitations placed on their activities were that they could not interfere in any way with the "peace and tranquility of international conference activities and premises," and that they could not hold a press conference. Their contacts with individual members of the press were not restricted, however.

The Americans indicated that they would remain in Helsinki for a few more days to answer inquiries regarding the status of the Baltic states and the circumstances of their incarceration.

The following U.S. citizens were involved:

Joseph Kestutis Valiunas
Uldis Ivars Grava
Ilmar Pleer
John B. Genys
Egle B. Zilionis
Peter John Vileisis

Appendix 1

LATVIANS IN AMERICA ACCORDING TO 1970 CENSUS DATA

(Source: U.S. Department of Commerce, Bureau of Census. 1970 Census
of Population: Characteristics of the Population. Washington, D.C.: U.S.
Government Printing Office, 1973.)

State	Foreign-Born Latvians	Nationals of Foreign or Mixed Parentage	Total No. of Latvians
Alabama	14	137	151
Alaska	14	34	48
Arizona	222	223	445
Arkansas	47	13	60
California	4,481	5,288	9,769
Colorado	383	294	677
Connecticut	1,245	1,271	2,516
Delaware	192	145	337
District of Columbia	165	186	351
Florida	971	1,580	2,551
Georgia	159	389	548
Hawaii	38	72	110
Idaho	21	14	35
Illinois	4,221	4,097	8,318
Indiana	1,002	615	1,617
Iowa	451	331	782
Kansas	67	158	225
Kentucky	73	178	251
Louisiana	58	58	116
Maine	70	81	151
Maryland	847	1,793	2,640
Massachusetts	2,263	2,837	5,100
Michigan	2,994	1,941	4,935
Minnesota	1,509	1,008	2,517
Mississippi	76	118	194
Missouri	169	315	484
Montana	78	8	86
Nebraska	602	314	916
Nevada	49	88	137
New Hampshire	74	125	199
New Jersey	2,247	2,917	5,164
New Mexico	33	54	87
New York	7,580	8,853	16,433

State	Foreign-Born Latvians	Nationals of Foreign or Mixed Parentage	Total No. of Latvians
North Carolina	174	161	335
North Dakota	69	30	99
Ohio	2,474	2,110	4,584
Oklahoma	170	147	317
Oregon	395	287	682
Pennsylvania	2,080	2,866	4,946
Rhode Island	148	197	345
South Carolina	26	99	125
South Dakota	83	84	167
Tennessee	107	135	242
Texas	354	667	1,021
Utah	3	21	24
Vermont	57	38	95
Virginia	301	555	856
Washington	1,189	675	1,864
West Virginia	26	80	106
Wisconsin	1,636	1,013	2,649
Wyoming	0	6	6
Total	41,707	44,706	86,413

Appendix 2

CENTRAL LATVIAN ORGANIZATIONS IN THE U.S.A.

NATIONAL ORGANIZATIONS IN THE U.S.A.

American Latvian Association in the United States, Inc.
American Latvian Catholic Association
American Latvian Relief Fund, Inc.
American Latvian Youth Association
Association of Latvian Credit Unions
Association of Latvian Fraternities
Association of Latvian Physicians and Dentists
Association of Latvian Song Festivals
Association of Latvian Sororities
Association of Latvian Student Unions
Latvian Artists' Group
Latvian Choir Association
Latvian Humanities and Social Sciences Association
Latvian Officers' Association
Latvian Press Association
Latvian Society of Foresters
Latvian Society of Jurists
Latvian Society of Lāčplēsis
Latvian Welfare Organization Daugavas Vanagi

LOCAL ORGANIZATIONS IN THE UNITED STATES

Religious Congregations   Social and Cultural Organizations

CALIFORNIA

Latvian Evangelical Lutheran Church
of Northern California (Rev. A.
Ernstsons)

Latvian Association of Southern
California

Latvian Evangelical Lutheran Church
of Oakland (Rev. G. Kņezs-Kņezin-
skis)

Latvian Society of Northern California

Latvian Evangelical Lutheran Church
of San Diego

Latvian Evangelical Lutheran Church
of Southern California (Rev. E.
Caune)

Latvian Evangelical Lutheran Church
of Peace in Los Angeles (Rev. O.
Kleinbergs)

| Religious Congregations | Social and Cultural Organizations |

COLORADO

Latvian Evangelical Lutheran Church of Denver and
Latvian Evangelical Lutheran Church of Colorado Springs (Rev. Ž. Upīte)

Latvian Association of Colorado Springs
Latvian Club of Denver

CONNECTICUT

Latvian Evangelical Lutheran Church of Manchester and
Latvian Evangelical Lutheran Church of Stamford (Rev. K. Freimanis)
Latvian Evangelical Lutheran Church of Willimantic (Rev. V. Rolle)
Latvian Catholic Organization of Willimantic

Latvian Society of Connecticut

DELAWARE

Latvian Evangelical Lutheran Church, Wilmington (Dr. A. Ziedonis, Jr.)

DISTRICT OF COLUMBIA

Latvian Evangelical Lutheran Church of Washington, D.C. (Rev. A. Veinbergs)
Latvian Baptist Society (Rev. A. Klaupiks)

Washington, D.C. Latvian Society
Latvian Women's Club of Washington, D.C.

FLORIDA

Latvian Evangelical Lutheran Church of St. Petersburg

Latvian Society of St. Petersburg
Latvian Society of Southern Florida

ILLINOIS

Latvian Evangelical Lutheran Zion Church of Chicago (Rev. V. Vārsbergs)
St. John's Latvian Evangelical Lutheran Church of Chicago (Rev. G. Straumanis)

Latvian Society of Chicago
Association of Latvian Organizations of Chicago

Religious Congregations   Social and Cultural Organizations

ILLINOIS (cont'd)

Latvian Evangelical Lutheran Church
of Peace of Chicago (Rev. H. Sudārs)
St. Paul's Latvian Evangelical Luther-
an Church of Maywood (Rev. M.
Ķirsons)
Latvian Evangelical Lutheran Zion
Church of Chicago, Joliet Branch
Latvian Catholic Congregation of Chi-
cago (Rev. B. Baginskis)
Latvian Dievturi in Chicago

INDIANA

Latvian Evangelical Lutheran Church   Latvian Society of Indiana (Indian-
of Indianapolis (Rev. P. Nesaule)   apolis)
Indiana Latvian Catholic Association   Latvian Community Center, Inc.
in Indianapolis (Rev. A. Grosbergs)   (Indianapolis
Latvian Evangelical Lutheran First
Church of Indianapolis (Rev. T.
Gulbis)

IOWA

Latvian Evangelical Lutheran Church   Latvian Society of Iowa in Des
in Des Moines (Rev. H. Jesifers)   Moines
Latvian Catholic Church in Des Moines
(Rev. L. Vārna)

KENTUCKY

                                             Latvian Club of Kentucky in Louis-
                                             ville

MASSACHUSETTS

Latvian Evangelical Lutheran Church   American National Latvian League,
of Jamaica Plain (Rev. Fr. Ruperts)   Inc. in Jamaica Plain
Latvian Evangelical Lutheran Trinity   American Latvian Theater Troupe
Church of Massachusetts (Rev. K.   of Boston
Kampe)
Latvian Evangelical Lutheran Church
of Massachusetts (Rev. A. Galiņš)

<u>Religious Congregations</u>   <u>Social and Cultural Organizations</u>

MASSACHUSETTS (cont'd)

Latvian Evangelical Lutheran Mis-
sion Church of Massachusetts
(Rev. N. Ozols)
Latvian Baptist Community of Boston
(Rev. E. Spigulis)
Latvian Catholic Community in Bos-
ton

MICHIGAN

Latvian Evangelical Lutheran Church
of Detroit (Rev. J. Lazda)

Latvian Evangelical Lutheran Church
of Grand Haven (Rev. K. Hermanis)

Latvian Evangelical Lutheran Church
of Grand Rapids (Rev. K. Hermanis)

Latvian Evangelical Lutheran Church
of Kalamazoo (Rev. A. Piebalgs)

Latvian Evangelical Lutheran Church
of Lansing (Rev. J. Turks)

St. Paul's Latvian Evangelical Lutheran Church of Detroit (Rev. V.
Līventāls)

Unity Latvian Evangelical Lutheran
Church of Grand Rapids (Rev. J.
Lazda)

Latvian Catholic Community of Detroit

Latvian Association of Detroit
Latvian Society of Grand Rapids
Latvian Club of Saginaw
Kalamazoo Latvian Society
Latvian Choir <u>Dziesmu Vairogs</u>

MINNESOTA

Latvian Evangelical Lutheran Christ
Church in Minneapolis (Rev. M.
Gulbis)

Latvian Evangelical Lutheran Church
of Minneapolis and St. Paul (Rev.
M. Ozoliņš)

Latvian Evangelical Lutheran Jesus
Church of Minneapolis (Rev. E.
Ķiploks)

Latvian Association of Minnesota

Religious Congregations | Social and Cultural Organizations

MISSISSIPPI

Latvian Evangelical Lutheran Church
of Senatobia (Rev. P. Nesaule)

MISSOURI

Latvian Evangelical Lutheran Church
of St. Louis (Rev. I. Kalniņš)

Latvian Society of St. Louis

NEBRASKA

Latvian Evangelical Lutheran Church
of Lincoln (Rev. H. Jesifers)
Latvian Evangelical Lutheran Church
of St. John in Lincoln (Rev. K. Bū-
manis)
Latvian Evangelical Lutheran Church
of Omaha (Rev. J. Dzirnis)

Latvian Society of Lincoln
Latvian Society of Omaha

NEW JERSEY

Latvian Evangelical Lutheran Church
of Elizabeth and Newark (Rev. T.
Vēdzele)
Latvian Evangelical Lutheran Church
of New Brunswick and Lakewood
(Rev. Ž. Kristbergs)
Latvian Evangelical Lutheran Church
of Seabrook

Latvian Society of Jew Jersey
The Association of Latvian Organ-
izations in New Jersey
Latvian American Republican Na-
tional Committee
Latvian National Center, New
Brunswick Chapter

NEW YORK

Buffalo Latvian Evangelical Lutheran
Church (Rev. J. Vējiņš)
Hudson Area Latvian Evangelical Lu-
theran Church (Rev. Kr. Valters,
Sr.)
Latvian Evangelical Lutheran Church
of New York (Revs. R. Zariņš, A.
Ozols, O. Gulbis)
Latvian Evangelical Lutheran Church
of Poughkeepsie (Rev. A. Anšēvics)

Albany Latvian Club
Latvian Society of Syracuse
Poughkeepsie Latvian Society
Council of American Latvian Or-
ganizations in New York
Latvian Society of New York

Religious Congregations   Social and Cultural Organizations

NEW YORK (cont'd)

Latvian Evangelical Lutheran Church
  of Schenectady (Rev. Kr. Valters,
  Sr.)
St. John's Latvian Evangelical Luther-
  an Church of Long Island (Rev. D.
  Grauds)
Latvian Evangelical Lutheran Christ
  Church of Syracuse (Rev. T. Zīrāks)
Latvian Evangelical Lutheran Church
  of Syracuse (Rev. J. Vējiņš)
New York Latvian Catholic American-
  Latvian Association Members
New York Latvian Catholic Society

NORTH DAKOTA

Latvian Evangelical Lutheran Group   Latvian Society of North Dakota
  of Minot (Rev. F. Kramiņš)   in Minot

OHIO

Latvian Evangelical Lutheran Church   Latvian Society of Cleveland
  of Cleveland (Rev. L. Grendze)   Latvian Society of Youngstown
Latvian Evangelical Lutheran Church   American Latvian Association
  of Columbus (Rev. V. Klīve)   Branch of Cleveland
Latvian Evangelical Lutheran Church   Columbus Latvian Society
  of Dayton (Rev. J. Osis)   Toledo Latvian Society
Latvian Evangelical Lutheran Church
  of Canton (Rev. H. Jurjāns)
Latvian Evangelical Lutheran Church
  of Martin Luther (Rev. K. Briedis)
Latvian Evangelical Lutheran Church
  of Peace
Latvian Catholic Society of Cleveland
  (Rev. A. Galdikovskis)

OREGON

Latvian Evangelical Lutheran Church   Latvian Association in Oregon
  of Oregon (Rev. J. Cilnis)   (Portland)

Religious Congregations	Social and Cultural Organizations

PENNSYLVANIA

Latvian Evangelical Lutheran Church
of Bucks County (Rev. A. Reinsons)
Latvian Evantelical Lutheran Church
of Philadelphia
St. John's Latvian Evangelical Lutheran Church of Philadelphia
Latvian Evangelical Lutheran Church
of Pittsburgh (Rev. K. Briedis)
Bucks' County Latvian Baptist Community (Rev. F. Čiekurs)
Philadelphia Latvian Catholic Community

Latvian Society of Lancaster and
Vicinity
Philadelphia Society of Free Letts
Latvian Society of Pittsburgh

SOUTH DAKOTA

Latvian Society of Sioux Falls

VIRGINIA

Latvian Catholic Organization of Washington, D.C. and vicinity (Rev. A.
Justs)

Latvian Society of Virginia (Rich-
mond)

WASHINGTON

Latvian Evangelical Lutheran Church
of Seattle (Rev. R. Āboliņš)
Latvian Evangelical Lutheran Church
of Tacoma (Rev. E. Mačs)

Latvian Association of Washington
in Seattle, with chapters in
Tacoma, Longview, Spokane,
and other cities

WISCONSIN

Latvian Evangelical Lutheran Church
of Martin Luther in Fond du Lac
St. John's Latvian Evangelical Luther-
an Church of Milwaukee (Rev. A.
Kalnājs)
Latvian Evangelical Lutheran Church
of Christ in Milwaukee (Rev. J.
Meistars)
Latvian Evangelical Lutheran Church
of Milwaukee (Rev. E. Putniņš)
Milwaukee Latvian Catholic Community

Latvian House of Milwaukee, Inc.

Appendix 3

SELECTED BIBLIOGRAPHY

History

Andersons, Edgar. Cross Road Country: Latvia. Waverly, Iowa: Latvju Grāmata, 1953.

Babris, Peter. Baltic Youth Under Communism. Arlington Heights, Ill.: Research Publishers, 1967.

Baltic Refugees and Displaced Persons. London: Boreas Publishing Co., Ltd., 1947

The Baltic States 1940-1972. Documentary Background and Survey of Developments Presented to the European Security and Cooperation Conference. Stockholm: The Baltic Committee in Scandinavia, 1972.

Berkis, Alexander. The History of the Duchy of Courland, 1561-1795. Townson, Md.: Paul M. Harrod Co., 1969

Berkis, Alexander. The Reign of Duke James in Courland, 1638-1682. Lincoln: Vaidava, 1960.

Berzins, Alfreds. The Tragedy of Latvia. Beirut: Photo Press, 1960.

Berzins, Alfreds. The Two Faces of Co-Existence. New York: Robert Speller & Sons, 1967.

Berzins, Alfreds. The Unpunished Crime. New York: Robert Speller & Sons, 1962.

Bilmanis, Alfred. Baltic Essays. Washington, D.C.: The Latvian Legation, 1945.

Bilmanis, Alfred. A History of Latvia. Princeton: Princeton University Press, 1951.

Bilmanis, Alfred. Latvia as an Independent State. Washington, D.C.: The Latvian Legation, 1947.

Bilmanis, Alfred. Latvian-Russian Relations. Documents. Washington, D.C.: The Latvian Legation, 1944.

Bilmanis, Alfred. Law and Courts in Latvia. Washington, D.C.: The Latvian Legation, 1946.

Blodnieks, Adolfs. The Undefeated Nation. New York: Robert Speller & Sons, 1960.

Carson, George B. Jr., ed. Latvia: An Area Study. New Haven: Human Relations Area Files, Inc., 1956.

Gimbutas, Marija. The Balts. New York: Praeger, 1963.

Goldhagen, Erich, ed. Ethnic Minorities in the Soviet Union. New York: Praeger, 1968.

Graham, Malbone W. Jr. New Governments of Eastern Europe. New York: Henry Holt & Co., 1927.

Grant-Watson, Herbert A. The Latvian Republic: The Struggle for Freedom. London: G. Allen & Unwin, 1956

Journal of the Baltic Studies. Brooklyn, N.Y.: Association for the Advancement of Baltic Studies.

Kalme, Albert. Total Terror: An Expose of Genocide in the Baltics. New York: Appleton-Century-Crofts, 1951.

Kavass, I., & A. Sprudzs, eds. Baltic States: A Study of their Origin and National Development: Their Seizure and Incorporation into the USSR. Third Interim Report of the Select Committee on Communist Aggression, House of Representatives, 83rd Congress, Second Session, 1954. Buffalo: Wm. S. Hein & Co., 1972.

King, Gundar J. Economic Policies in Occupied Latvia: A Manpower Management Study. Tacoma: Pacific Lutheran University Press, 1965.

Latvian Information Bulletin. Washington, D.C.: The Latvian Legation

Newman, W.P. Edward. Britain and the Baltic. London, 1930.

Page, Stanley W. The Formation of the Baltic States. Cambridge: Harvard University Press, 1959.

Pick, Frederic W. The Baltic Nations. London: Boreas Publishing Co., Ltd., 1945.

Rei, August. The Drama of the Baltic Peoples. Stockholm: Kirjastus Vaba Eesti, 1970.

Rutkis, Janis, ed. Latvia: Country and People. Stockholm: Latvian National Foundation in Scandinavia, 1967.

Silde, Adolfs. The Profits of Slavery: Baltic Forced Laborers and De-
    portees Under Stalin and Khrushchev. Stockholm: Latvian National
    Foundation in Scandinavia, 1958.

Silde, Adolfs. Resistance Movement in Latvia. Stockholm: Latvian Na-
    tional Foundation in Scandinavia, 1972.

Spekke, Arnolds. The Ancient Amber Routes and the Geographic Discovery
    of the Eastern Baltic. Stockholm: Goppers, 1957.

Spekke, Arnolds. Balts and Slavs: Their Early Relations. Washington,
    D.C.: Alpha Printing Co., 1965.

Spekke, Arnolds. History of Latvia: An Outline. Stockholm: Goppers,
    1951.

Spekke, Arnolds. Latvia and the Baltic Problem: Sketch of Recent History.
    London: Latvian Information Bureau, Latvian Legation, 1954.

Sprudzs, Adolfs & Armins Rusis. Res Baltica: A Collection of Essays in
    Honor of the Memory of Dr. Alfreds Bilmanis (1887-1948). Leyden:
    A. W. Sijthoff, 1968.

Svabe, Arveds. The Story of Latvia and Her Neighbours: A Historical
    Survey. Edinburgh: Scottish League for European Freedom, 1946.

Swettenham, John A. The Tragedy of the Baltic States: A Report Compiled
    from Official Documents and Eyewitness Stories. London: Hollis and
    Carter, 1952.

Tarulis, Albert N. American-Baltic Relations, 1919-1922: The Struggle
    Over Recognition. Washington, D.C.: Catholic University of America
    Press, 1965.

Tarulis, Albert N. Soviet Policy Toward the Baltic States, 1918-1940.
    South Bend, Ind.: University of Notre Dame Press, 1959.

World Federation of Free Latvians. Memoranda on Reestablishing Free-
    dom and Independence in Latvia in Connection with the European Secur-
    ity and Cooperation Conference. Washington, D.C.: World Federa-
    tion of Free Latvians, 1973.

Language and Literature

Aigars, Peteris. The Red Train. Translated from the Latvian original by
    W.K. Matthews. Lubeck, West Germany: Kursa, 1951.

Andrups, J., and V. Kalve. Latvian Literature. Stockholm: Zelta Abele, 1954.

Budina-Lazdina, T. Teach Yourself Latvian. London: The English Universities, 1966.

Eglitis, Anslavs. Ajurjonga. Translated from Latvian by L. Parks. Stockholm: Daugava, 1955.

Endzelins, Janis. Comparative Phonology and Morphology of the Baltic Languages. Hague, Netherlands: Mouton, 1971.

"The First Conference on Baltic Literatures, Part I." Lituanus, Vol. 16, No. 1 (Spring 1970).

"The First Conference on Baltic Literatures, Part II." Lituanus, Vol.16, No. 2 (Summer 1970).

Lesins, Knuts. The Wine of Eternity. Minneapolis: University of Minnesota Press, 1957. (Short stories from the Latvian.)

Matthews, W.K. A Century of Latvian Poetry. London: John Calder, 1957.

Mezezers, Valdis. God and Man" Sermons and Meditations. New York: Vantage Press, 1956.

Mezezers, Valdis. The Great Light: Sermons and Meditations. Boston: The Christopher Publishing House, 1957.

Millers, Reinhold. Teenangel. New York: Echo Publishers, 1971.

Millers, Reinhold. Time Exile. New York: Echo Publishers, 1972.

Rubulis, Aleksis. Baltic Literature: A Survey of Finnish, Estonian, Latvian and Lithuanian Literatures. South Bend, Ind.: University of Notre Dame Press, 1970.

Rubulis, Aleksis. Latvian Literature: An Anthology. Toronto: Daugavas Vanagi, 1964.

Skalbe, Karlis. Pussy's Water Mill. A Fairy Tale. Translated from Latvian by W.K. Matthews. Stockholm: Zelta Abele, 1952.

Zeps, Valdis J. Latvian and Finnic Linguistic Convergences. Bloomington, Ind.: Indiana University Press, 1963.

Ziverts, Martins. The Jester. Translated from Latvian by Lucija Berzina-Felsberga. Sidney, Australia: Sala Press, 1964.

Ziverts, Martins. The Ore. Translated from Latvian by Lucija Berzina-Felsberga. Sidney, Australia: Sala Press, 1968.

Articles

"Americans of Latvian Lineage." The Book of America's Making Exposition, October 29-November 12, 1921, New York.

Andersons, Edgar. "The British Policy Toward the Baltic States 1918-1920." Journal of Central European Affairs, Vol. XIX, No. 3 (October 1959), pp. 276-289.

Andersons, Edgar. "Toward the Baltic Entente - the Initial Phase." Pro Baltica. Melanges dedies a Kaarel R. Pusta. Stockholm: Publications du Comite des amis de K.R. Pusta, 1965.

Andersons, Edgar. "Toward the Baltic Union - the Initial Phase." Lituanus, Vol. XIII, No. 1 (Spring, 1968).

Andersons, Edgar. "Toward the Baltic Union, 1920-1927." Lituanus, Vol. XII, No. 2 (Summer, 1966).

Andersons, Edgar. "Toward the Baltic Union, 1927-1934." Lituanus, Vol. XIII, No. 1 (Spring, 1967).

Andersons, Edgar. "Through the Baltic Gate." The Baltic Review, No. XXXIII (January, 1967).

Andersons, Edgar. An Undeclared Naval War." Journal of Central European Affairs, Vol. XXII, No. 1 (April 1962).

Andersons, Edgar. "The USSR Trades with Latvia: The Treaty of 1927." Slavic Review, Vol. XXI, No. 2 (June 1962).

Dinbergs, Anatol. "Soviet Occupation of Latvia has no Legal Ground." Washington, D.C.: Latvian Information Bulletin, October, 1964.

Dreifelds, Juris. "Characteristics and Trends of Two Demographic Variables in the Latvian S.S.R." Bulletin of Baltic Studies, Vol. VIII (1971), pp. 10-17.

Dzilleja, Karlis, "Schools and Educational Standards in Occupied Latvia."
    The Baltic Review, Vol. XIV (August 1958). pp. 3-32.

Ekmanis, Rolf. "After Eighteen Years of Captivity: The Threat of Revi-
    sionism in Soviet-occupied Baltic States." International Peasant Union
    Bulletin, February 1959, pp. 21-24.

Ezergailis, Andrew. "The Bolsehvization of the Latvian Social Democratic
    Party." Canadian Slavic Studies, Vol. 1, No. 2 (1957), pp. 238-252.

Ezergailis, Andrew. "1917 in Latvia: The Bolshevik Year." Canadian Sla-
    vic Studies, Vol. III, No. 4 (1969), pp. 646-662.

Gwertzman, Bernard. "Latvian Protest Held Authentic." The New York
    Times, February 27, 1972.

Hazners, Vilis. "Current Events - Latvia." The Baltic Review, Vol.
    XVIV (March 1960), pp. 43-47.

Hunczak, Taras. "Operation Winter: and the Struggle for the Baltic."
    East European Quarterly, Vol. IV, No. 1 (1970), pp. 40-57.

Kalnins, Bruno. "The Position of Minorities in the Soviet Union." Bulletin
    of Baltic Studies, Vol. VIII (1971), pp. 3-9.

King, Gundar. "Management of the Economy and Political Power: The
    Latvian Case." Lituanus, Vol. 14, No. 3 (1968), pp. 54-72.

Kratins, Ojars. "Recent Developments in Latvian Fiction." Slavic and
    East European Journal. Vol. 2 (1972), pp. 193-205.

Latvia. In Commemoration of the 50th Anniversary of the Declaration of
    Independence of the Republic of Latvia. Washington, D.C.: American
    Latvian Association in the United States, Inc., 1968.

"Latvian Communists Appeal to West." The Daily Telegraph, February
    7, 1972.

Machray, Robert. "British Policy in the Baltic." Fortnightly, CXXIV,
    New Series (October 1933), p. 403.

Roucek, Joseph S. "Latvians in the United States." Baltic Countries, II.
    Torun-Gdinia, 1936.

Roucek, Joseph S. "New Immigration: Eastern European States. Latvian
    Americans." One America, 1949, 1952.

Shabad, Theodore. "Migrants Worry Estonia, Latvia." The New York Times, March 13, 1972.

Schnorf, Richard Arthur. "Problem of International Morality as Represented by the Baltic States." Washington, D.C.: The American University, October 1963. (Master's Thesis).

Skreija, Andris. "Interests and Interest Orientations of Latvian Refugees as Reflected in their Newspapers." Lexington, Ky.: University of Kentucky, 1964. (Unpublished)

Thomson, Erik. "Baltic Tragedy." Central Europe Journal, 9/10 (1971), pp. 310-318.

Veidemanis, Juris. "Latvian Settlers in Wisconsin: A Comparative View." Wisconsin Magazine of History, 1962, Vol. 45.

Veidemanis, Juris. "Neglected Areas in the Sociology of Immigrants and Ethnic Groups in North America." The Sociological Quarterly, Vol. IV (1963) pp. 323-333.

Veidemanis, Juris. "Social Change: Latvian Major Value-Systems at Home, as Refugees, and as Immigrants." Madison: University of Wisconsin, 1961. (Unpublished Ph. D. Thesis)

Veidemanis, Juris. "A Twentieth Century Pioneer Settlement: Latvians in Lincoln County." Journal of the Midcontinent American Studies Association. Vol. IV (1963)

Veidemanis, Juris. "Two Generations of Mental Isolation: Latvians in Northern Wisconsin." The Wisconsin Sociologist, 1960.

Viksnins, George J. "The Latvian Economy 1920-1959." Philadelphia: University of Pennsylvania, 1960. (Unpublished Master's Thesis)

Williams, Maynard Owen. "Latvia, Home of the Letts." The National Geographic Magazine, Vol. XLVI, No. 4 (October 1924).

Ziverts, Karlis. "The Population of Latvia under Soviet Occupation." East and West (London), No. 4, 1955.

Bibliographies

Jegers, Benjamins. Bibliography of Latvian Publications Outside Latvia 1940-1960: Vol. I: Books and Pamphelts. Stockholm: Daugava, 1968.

Jegers, Benjamins. Bibliography of Latvian Publications Outside Latvia
1940-1960: Vol. II: Serials, Music, Maps, Programs, Catalogues.
Stockholm: Daugava, 1972.

Ozols, Zelma Aleksandra. Latvia: A Selected Bibliography. Washington,
D.C.: K. Karusa, 1963.

Miscellaneous

Andersons, Edgar, Rimvydas Silbajoris & Arvids Ziedonis, eds. Second
Conference on Baltic Studies: Summary of Proceedings. Norman,
Okla.: Association for the Advancement of Baltic Studies, the Univer-
sity of Oklahoma, 1971.

Bernholm, Anders. Riga Today: With the Swedish Coastal Fleet in Riga.
Stockholm: Latvian National Fund in the Scandinavian Countries, 1956.

Dunn, Stephen. Cultural Processes in the Baltic Area Under Soviet Rule.
Berkeley: University of California Press, 1966.

Ivask, Ivar, ed. First Conference on Baltic Studies: Summary of Proceedings. Tacoma, Wash.: Association for the Advancement of Baltic
Studies, Pacific Lutheran University, 1969.

Norvilis, P., and J. Silins. Latvian Art on Display. Washington, D.C.:
American Latvian Association in the United States, Inc., 1968.

Platbarzdis, A. Coins and Notes of Estonia, Latvia, Lithuania. Stockholm:
Numismatika Bokforlaget, 1968.

Latvian Periodicals

Akadēmiskā Dzīve ("Academic Life"). Indianapolis, Ind.; A. Karps, Ed.,
(1958-).

ALA Vēstis (ALA "News"). Quarterly publication; Washington, D.C.:
The American Latvian Association; Adolfs Lejiņš, ed. (1972-).

ALA Žurnāls (ALA "Journal"). Quarterly publication; Washington, D.C.:
The American Latvian Association; Alīda Cīrule, ed. (1970-).

Amerikas Latviešu Apvienības Kultūras Birojs. ("American Latvian Association, Bureau of Culture") Biļetēns. ("Bulletin"). Washington, D.C.;
American Latvian Association; P. Norvilis, ed. (1958-).

Amerikas latviešu humanitāro zinātņu asociācija ("American Latvian Association for Humanities") Apkārtraksts ("Bulletin"). New York, (1956-1960)

Amerikas latviešu jaunatnes apvienība ("American Latvian Youth Association") Raksti ("Essays"). New York; M. Austriņa,H. Nordens, et al., eds. (1952-1954).

Amerikas Vēstnesis ("American Herald"). Boston; O. Liepiņš, ed., (1955-1960).

Atstari ("Reflections of Rays"). Grand Rapids, Mich.; Latvian Youth Group in Grand Rapids, Mich.; J. Gorsvans, ed. (1951-1959).

Atvase ("Offspring"). Washington, D.C.: Latvian Youth Group of Washington, D.C.; J. Ozoliņš, M. Freivalds and I. Birznieks, eds. (1953-1956).

Ausma ("Dawn") Boston: Latvian Literary Committee of Boston; J. Daugmanis, ed. (1941-1944).

Ausma ("Dawn"). Indianapolis: Latvian Society of Indiana; V. Burģis et al, eds. (1952-1957).

Avots Prērijā ("Stream in the Prairie"). Sioux Falls, S.D., and Minneapolis, Minn.; E. Ķiploks et al, eds. (1951-1956).

The Baltic Review. New York: Committees for a Free Estonia, Latvia and Lithuania; A. Berzins et al, eds. (1953-   ).

Bitītes Kalendārs ("A Calendar for the Children").

Brīvības Talcinieks ("A Helper for Freedom"). Brooklyn, N.Y.; Flushing, N.Y., Maywood, Ill.: American Latvian Youth Association; A. Osis, ed. (1957-1960).

Ceļa Biedrs ("Companion"). Minneapolis: Sējējs; O. Gulbis and J. Strautnieks, eds. (1956-   ).

Daugavas Vanagu Mēnešraksts ("Daugavas Vanagi Monthly"). Toronto: Daugavas Vanagi Publishing Co.; Vilis Hāzners, ed. (1953-   ).

Drauga Vēsts ("News from a Friend"). New York: First Latvian Baptist Congregation in New York; K. Purgailis, ed. (1942-1947).

Dzelzceļnieks ("Railwayman"). Bronx, N.Y.: Latvian Railwaymen's Association; E. Krieviņš, et al, eds. (1953-   ).

Dzirkstelīte ("The Little Spark"). Cleveland: Latvian Boy Scout Troup Daugava of Cleveland; Z. Tobiens, ed. (1956-1962).

Jaunā Gaita ("Latvian Youth Magazine"). Lincoln, Neb., Kalamazoo, Mich.,
Toronto: American Latvian Youth Association and Celinieks; L. Zand-
bergs, , et al, eds. (1955-). Currently Hamilton, Ont., Canada:
Latvian Youth Literary Society Celinieks.

Jaunais Laikmets ("The New Era"). Hackettstown, N.J.; R. Grava, ed.
(1952-).

Jaunās Balsis ("The New Voices"). North Hollywood, Calif.: Latvian
Youth Group of Southern California; O. Stumbrs, et al, eds. (1954-
1958).

The Journal of Baltic Studies. Quarterly publication in English; New York:
Association for the Advancement of Baltic Studies; Dr. Arvids Ziedonis,
Jr., ed. (1970-).

Katolu vēstis latviešiem ("Catholic News for Latvians"). Louisville, Ky.;
R. Pudans, ed. (1950-1952).

Kollekcionārs ("Philatelist"). Lincoln, Neb.: Vaidava; A Petrevics, ed.
(1960-).

Kontrapunkts (Musical Counterpoint). Kalamazoo, Mich.: Dziesmu Vairogs; J. Avotiņš, et al, eds. (1951-).

Kristīgā Balss ("Christian Voice"). Toronto, Canada; R. Eksteins, et al,
eds. (1950-).

Labietis. Chicago; A. Brastins, ed. (1955-).

Laikmets ("Era"). Minneapolis: Sēlzemnieks; K. Miķelsons, et al, eds.
(1953-).

Laiks ("Time"). New York: Grāmatu Draugs; H. Rudzītis, et al, eds.
(1949-). (The most extensively read newspaper in the U.S.A. among
Latvians and by Latvians in the free world -- published twice a week.)

Lāpa ("Torch"). Tacoma, Wash.: Latvian Youth Group in Tacoma; G.
Abolins, B. Vidmane and G. Valdnieks, eds. (1955-1957).

Latvian Bulletin. New York: Latvian American Information Center; O.K.
Armstrong, A. Berzins, et al, eds. (1951-1953).

Latvian Information Bulletin. Washington, D.C.: The Press Bureau of the
Latvian Legation (1940-).

Latviešu Akadēmiskās Ziņas ("Latvian Academic Review"). Bronx, N.Y.:
P. Norvilis, ed. (1953-).

Latviešu Juristu Raksti ("Publications of Latvian Lawyers"). Kalamazoo,
Mich.: Kent Association of Latvian Lawyers; K. Ozoliņš, ed. (1959-).

Latvija Amerikā ("Latvia in America"). Toronto: Latvian Relief Organization Daugavas Vanagi; K. Sidars, et al, eds. (1951-).

Latvija Šodien ("Latvia Today"). Annual publication; Washington, D.C.:
World Federation of Free Latvians; Dr. Ilgvars J. Spilners, ed.
(1972-).

Latvijas Brīvībai ("Freedom of Latvia"). New York; V. Māsens, A. Bļod-
nieks, A. Bērziņš, eds. (1952-).

Latvju Jaunā Baznīca ASV (Latvian Church in US) Pine Brook, N.J.: R.
Grava, B. Kalniņš, et al, eds. (1952-).

Latvju Mūzika ("Latvian Music"). Kalamazoo, Mich.: Latvian Choir Association, Inc.; Valentīns Bērzkalns, ed. (1968-).

Latvju Sieviete (Latvian Woman) Minneapolis, Minn: Sēļzemnieka Apgāds;
K. Miķelsons, et al, eds. (1952).

Latvju Žurnāls (Latvian Journal) New York: O. Liepiņš et al, eds. (1951-
1956).

Linkolnas Vēstnesis (Lincoln Herald) Lincoln, Neb.: Latvian Evangelical
Lutheran Church of Lincoln, Neb.; A. Pētersons, et al, eds. (1952-
1959).

Lituanus. Quarterly publication in English. Chicago: Lituanus Foundation,
Inc.; John A. Rackauskas, ed.

Mana Draudze (My Congregation). Newton Highlands, Mass.: Latvian
Baptist Congregation; V. Freimanis, ed. (1952-1961).

Mazputniņš (Latvian Children's Magazine) Toronto: Latvian Youth Literary Society, Ceļinieks. Laimonis and Līga Streips, eds., Morton
Grove, Ill. (1959-).

Modernie Rokdarbi (Modern Arts & Crafts) Waverly, Ohio: O. Dīķis.
A. Reinholds, ed. (1952-1954).

Mūsu Ceļš (Our Road) Lincoln, Neb.: Vaidava. (1956-1960).

Šacha Pasaule (Chess World - the Latvian Chess Magazine). Lincoln,
    Neb.: J. Pamiljenis, ed. (1954-   ).

Skaida (A Chip) New York: Latvian Boy Scouts, Rīga, Latvian Girl Scouts,
    Zilais Kalns; I. Eglīte, et al, eds.   (1956-1959).

Sporta Apskats (Sports Review) Toronto: Eds. G. Gubiņš, Toronto, G.
    Grieze, USA. (1956-   ).

Strēlnieks (The Soldier) New York: Latvian War Veterans; (1957-   ).

Tālavas Taurētājs (A Youth Magazine) Lincoln, Neb.: Tālavas Taurētājs;
    T. Dukāts, et al, eds. (1960)

Technikas Apskats (Review of Technology) Montreal, Canada: Latvian
    Engineer Association; A. Spurmanis, ed. (1954-   ).

Tilts (The Bridge) Minneapolis: Tilts; H. Skrastiņš, ed. (1949-   ).

Treji vārti ("Three Gates"). Bimonthly publication. Three Rivers, Mich.;
    Jānis Zariņš et al, eds. (1967-   ).

Trimdas Skola (School in Exile) A. Kurmis, E. Pētersons, eds. (1954-
    1964).

Trimdas Sports (Latvian Sports in Exile) Toronto: Council of Latvian
    Sports in Exile; P. Plīsis et al, eds. (1952-1956).

Ugunskurs (Camp Fire) Minneapolis: A. Lūsis, I. Kažociņš, et al, eds.
    (1948-1959)

Ugunskurs (Camp Fire) Cleveland: Latvian Baptist Youth Association; A.
    Kronbergs, et al, eds. (1956-1961).

Universitas-Trimdā (University in Exile) Stuttgart-Bad Canstatt, West
    Germany: A. Šilde, E. Rozītis, eds. (1954-   ). (A journal especially
    for students and graduates of universities who belong to Latvian fra-
    ternities and sororities.)

Zintis ("The Quarterly American Latvian Magazine for Art, Literature
    and Science"). Chicago: A. Kalnājs; H. B. Atoms et al, eds. (1960-
    1965).